Lausanne Occasional Paper 29

Spiritual Conflict in Today's Mission

A Report from the Consultation on "Deliver Us from Evil"

August 2000

Nairobi, Kenya

Tormod Engelsviken

Edited by A. Scott Moreau

Published by

Association of Evangelicals of Africa

Lausanne Committee for World Evangelization

The Lausanne Committee for World Evangelization (LCWE) is an international movement for the purpose of encouraging Christians and churches everywhere to pray, study, plan and work together for the evangelisation of the world.

Printed in the United States of America.

08 07 06 05 04 03 02 01   8 7 6 5 4 3 2 1

Copyediting: Beverle E. Wiggs. Typesetting and cover design: Richard Sears.

Available from:

Association of Evangelicals of Africa, P.O. Box 48332, Nairobi, Kenya
Tel: 254-2-720220, Fax: 254-2-713004, E-mail: adeyemo-aea@maf.or.ke

MARC Publications, 800 West Chestnut Avenue, Monrovia, California 91016-3198, U.S.A.

Library of Congress Cataloging-in-Publication Data
Engelsviken, Tormod.
   Spiritual conflict in today's mission : a report from the Consultation
on "Deliver Us from Evil," August 2000, Nairobi, Kenya / Tormod
Engelsviken ; edited by A. Scott Moreau.
      p. cm. — (Lausanne occasional paper ; 29)
Includes bibliographical references.
   ISBN 1-887983-24-4 (alk. paper)
   1. Missions—Theory—Congresses. 2. Consultation on "Deliver Us from
Evil" (2000 : Nairobi, Kenya) 3. Spiritual warfare—Congresses. 4.
Evangelicalism—Congresses. I. Moreau, A. Scott, 1955 – II. Title. III.
Series.
   BV2063 .E537 2001
   235'.4—dc21
                                                                2001003669

This book is printed on acid-free paper.

Contents

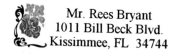

Preface

This Lausanne Occasional Paper (LOP) contains one person's perspective on the proceedings of the Consultation on "Deliver Us From Evil" held in Nairobi, Kenya, in August 2000. Space limitations preclude this LOP from presenting all that took place at the consultation. The main intention here is to focus on the overarching issues and to present the crucial ideas and viewpoints — as the author saw them.

This LOP draws extensively on the papers given, sometimes quoting them almost verbatim and at length without attribution. Even so, some rather radical abbreviations and editorial work have been required to fit the space allowed. For the full treatment of the consultation, including all papers presented in edited form, the reader is advised to consult the comprehensive volume, *Deliver Us from Evil*, to be published by World Vision under its MARC imprint.

We give credit to the authors and participants at the consultation for all significant contributions in this paper, and claim the blame for all the shortcomings. May God bless this work and the contributors!

Author: Tormod Engelsviken
Oslo, Norway April 2001

Editor: A. Scott Moreau
Wheaton, Illinois, USA April 2001

Introduction

The Theology and Strategy Working Group and the Intercessory Working Group of the Lausanne Committee for World Evangelization (LCWE), together with the Association of Evangelicals in Africa (AEA), convened a consultation on spiritual conflict August 16th-22nd 2000 in Nairobi, Kenya. The steering committee guiding this effort included Knud Jørgensen (chair), Tokunboh Adeyemo, Tormod Engelsviken, Scott Moreau, Bryant Myers, Birger Nygaard, Patrick Sookhdeo and Oddvar Søvik. The motto for the consultation was the prayer "Deliver Us from Evil" taken from the Lord's Prayer.

In the consultation, we sought a broad representation of the views and practices on the subject hoping that we might openly deal with the differences found within the evangelical community, that new insights might be gained from a broad and varied approach and that the new understandings achieved might be communicated among the various strands of spirituality through churches, organisations and networks. The participants included church and mission leaders, pastors and evangelists, and academics and practitioners from different churches and regions of the world (see Appendix A). The African setting of the consultation was strongly taken into account both in the planning of the programme and in the work of the consultation.

Background

In the last decade or so of the twentieth century, there has been a greatly heightened interest in this subject in evangelical circles. The reasons for this interest — and the controversy that sometimes accompanies it — are many and varied. Several trends have contributed:

- In a post-modern Western world, there has been a growing disillusionment with the purely rational or materialistic approach to modern life.

- In the church, there has been a serious decline in the numbers and fervour in mainline denominations that have been strongly influenced by this modern, rational approach.

- Through increased contact and co-operation in evangelisation between churches around the world, the experiences of churches in spiritual conflict in the non-Western world have impacted the views of the rest of the world church and created more openness to spiritual realities.

- Pentecostal and charismatic churches, with their openness to spiritual experiences, have grown greatly in almost all regions of the world.

- Changes in belief and practice in evangelical circles, fostered by new literature and teaching seminars, have disseminated a new vocabulary with prominence given to demons, spirits and other supernatural beings and how to deal with them on different levels.

- Violent ethnic conflicts have raised the question: How do we understand evil in the world today in the light of spiritual conflict?

Additionally, serious theological problems and questions for world evangelisation have been raised:

- The Christian ethic could be undermined where human responsibility is set aside by inappropriately attributing matters to demonic activity.

- The proper contextualisation of the gospel in a culture is neglected because the only category for answers to issues is spiritual warfare.

- The authority and sufficiency of Scripture may be called into question by the willingness to adopt ideas and practices that admittedly have little or no biblical basis.

- The question of proper hermeneutics in dealing with biblical teachings on demonic powers is being raised.

- The unity of the evangelical mission movement and the

willingness and ability of believers to co-operate are being undermined.

Faced with these and other challenges, the churches and their ministries have tended to fall into five categories:

1. Those who dismiss the idea of the real existence of a spirit world altogether;

2. Those who may believe in it in a theoretical sense, but are not aware of it in any practical way and have not, therefore, developed any practices related to it;

3. Those who have always had what they considered to be biblical views and prayer disciplines related to the spirit world and who dismiss the new approaches as unbiblical or theologically unsound;

4. Those who are aware of the spirit world, have absorbed and, to some degree, gone along with current changes — but still have questions and frustrations with some elements; and

5. Those who unquestioningly have accepted the new views and practices associated with spiritual warfare and practise it.

Purpose

Some of these concerns form the background of the calling together of this consultation. *The purpose of this consultation was therefore to develop an understanding of who the Enemy is, how he is working and how we can fight him in order to evangelise all peoples.*

Procedure

The purpose of the consultation was achieved by approaching the subject from four main trajectories: biblical and historical foundations, theological interpretations, contemporary and geographical contexts, and missional responses and strategies.

The consultation was opened by a keynote address by the Archbishop of the Anglican Church Province of Kenya, Dr David Gitari.

Over the course of one week, 12 plenary papers and 10 case studies from diverse ecclesial, professional, cultural and geographic perspectives were given at the consultation. We started each day with a Bible exposition on a pertinent topic or text.

Almost all of the plenary papers and case studies were made available in advance by means of the World Wide Web (WWW), at www.lausanne.org/dufe/, and e-mail in order for the participants and others to be able to read the papers and interact with the authors. Because all participants were expected to have read the papers beforehand, the presenters were able to give summaries and a significant amount of time was given to discussion to ensure that all voices were heard. The common work of participants resulted in a document that was unanimously approved at the end of the consultation (see Section 13).

1. The Biblical Foundation

A major contribution in the consultation to understand spiritual conflict in biblical perspective was made by Dr John Christopher Thomas. He pointed out, however, that the task of laying a biblical foundation for a theological discussion of spiritual conflict in the consultation would be an extremely difficult one. Thus, there needs to be an awareness that only a slice of the larger whole can be presented in order to deal with the issues at hand.

Origins of Affliction

By first focusing on the origins of affliction, a better understanding of spiritual conflict may be attained as the role of the Devil and demons in afflicting individuals is seen alongside other origins of illness, thereby preserving the tension of the biblical text itself on this topic. The New Testament identifies three primary causes of illness and/or infirmities: (1) God, (2) the Devil and/or demons and (3) what might most appropriately be called natural (or neutral) causes.

God as Origin of Illness

One of the points on which there is a great deal of agreement in the New Testament materials is that God is often attributed a role in the origins of illness. Generally speaking, the New Testament writers show little of the reluctance many modern students of the New Testament exhibit in assigning to God an active role in the affliction of individuals with disease and/or death. God's involvement is presented in a multi-faceted fashion. Specifically, infirmity and/or death can be used by God as (1) a pedagogical tool (1 Cor 11:29-30; Luke 1:20; Acts 9:8-9); (2) an instrument of punishment (Acts 12:19b-23; 13:6-12); (3) a means of spreading the gospel (John 9; Gal 4:13-14) and (4) a source of sanctification (2 Cor 12:7-10).

Far from simply being a source of healing, God can also be depicted as the origin or user of infirmity or death. When described in such a way, there always seem to be specific reasons for God's actions. God is seen to be sovereign, one who may act in ways that will achieve the Lord's will, a God who is to be approached with a holy fear. The New Testament writers did not always attribute infirmity to Satan, but worked with a more dialectical worldview where God could also afflict. Such an understanding suggests that God is not only able to use suffering indirectly, but can also take a more direct role in this activity.

The Devil and/or Demons as Source of Infirmity

The New Testament evidence is found primarily in the synoptic Gospels and in Acts. It may be divided into three main areas: (1) demon possession, (2) demonic affliction distinct from possession and (3) attack by Satan or sinister forces.

Demon Possession. There are several accounts of demon possession in the New Testament. The victims are described as being dominated by a demon or unclean spirit to the extent that they lose the ability to control or perform normal functions. At times, convulsions and other body responses prove to be so violent and uncontrollable that they place both the victims and those near them in danger of physical harm. In contrast to claims made both at the scholarly and popular level, the New Testament writers generally make a clear distinction between demon possession and illness.

Demonic Affliction. There are a few occasions where an infirmity is attributed to demonic activity without any suggestion that the afflicted person is under the control of an unclean spirit: Peter's mother-in-law (Luke 4:38-39), the woman with a spirit of infirmity (Luke 13:10-16) and Paul's thorn in the flesh (2 Cor 12:7). In each, a spirit afflicts the individual sufferer without indications of actual possession. Those who suffer in this way are not in need of exorcism (or deliverance) as much as healing.

Attacks on Messengers of God. There is some New Testament evidence that sinister forces could attack a messenger of God in an attempt to thwart God's way of salvation or the preaching of the gospel. Examples may include Paul's snakebite on Malta (Acts 28:1-6), Peter's opposition to Jesus' way of suffering and death (Matt 16:23), the Devil's temptation of Jesus himself (Matt 4:1-11) and possibly Judas' treason (John 13:27).

Infirmity and Natural Causes

A number of infirmities in the New Testament might best be described as owing their origin to neutral or natural causes. The vast majority of references to infirmities do not give any indication as to their origin. While it may be theoretically possible to attribute all these infirmities to the Devil or a world estranged from God or the effects of sin in the world, the texts themselves do not explicitly offer support for such a view.

Responses to Affliction

Given the various origins of and purposes for affliction and infirmity in the New Testament, the responses to it also take a variety of forms, including prayer, discernment, confession and intercession, exorcism and medicine.

Prayer

One of the more common responses is *prayer.* James 5 indicates that prayer plays an integral role in the healing of the sick. Paul's practice in 1 Corinthians 12 also indicates that prayer may have been his own habit in the face of infirmity. We may also assume that prayer had a place in the ministry of those with the gifts of healing and accompanied the laying on of hands. Peter raised Tabitha from the dead after prayer (Acts 9:40) and Mark 9:29 also suggests that prayer plays a crucial role in the disciples' casting out of demons.

Discernment

Since infirmities may have different causes, and even the same afflictions may be attributed to several causes, it is clear that *discernment* plays a crucial role in responding to them. This point may be illustrated by two attested categories: infirmity that results from sin and infirmity that results from demon possession. In cases of sin as the cause, it seems as if the sufferer himself may know the cause of illness (John 5:14; possibly also James 5:15-16). There is also a role for the Christian community in the discernment of sin as a cause for illness (1 Cor 11:27-32). The leaders of the church have a special responsibility in the discernment process. Both Peter and Paul exhibit this ability to discern (eg, Acts 5:1-11; 13:9-11).

Confession and Intercession

When sin stands behind an infirmity, one of the responses called for is *confession*. This response is made explicit in James 5. Confession is to be made to other members of the Christian community for the express purpose of intercession. The implication of this admonition is that such confession is to result in forgiveness and healing. Intercessory prayer is described as generally efficacious and has deep roots in New Testament spirituality. It is used in many different contexts.

Exorcism

The appropriate response to demon possession is *exorcism*, the authoritative expulsion of evil spirits by a command from Jesus, or in the name of Jesus and with the power of the Holy Spirit. There are several characteristic traits of the exorcism stories in the New Testament.

There is usually a direct dialogue between Jesus and the demon(s) in the possessed person. This dialogue is lacking in the healing stories because there is no demon to speak to. In the dialogues, demons know who Jesus is before people do: the Son of God who has come to end their dominion. Jesus also knows who and what the demons are. He expresses his authority over them through his words, and most of all through a direct command to leave the possessed. Jesus does not expel the demons in any other name; he does it on his own authority and by the Spirit of God. Beyond the dialogue in the Gospels, there are few criteria for the presence of an evil spirit in a human being except that the demons in different ways harm and control the people they possess. It is as if the need for criteria of possession was not felt in New Testament times simply because the phenomena were recognised on the basis of long experience. Finally, the exorcisms were always successful — the demons left and those who had been possessed were fully restored to normal life.

The exorcisms of Jesus must be understood within a larger framework of conflict between God and Satan. Satan's goal is especially to lead people away from God and generally to destroy God's good creation. One of the means of Satan, in his effort to destroy God's creation, is demon possession. The fact that possession exists is evidence of the power of Satan in this world. Therefore, the significance of exorcism is also clear. Jesus illuminates this: "Or how can anyone enter the strong man's house and carry off his property, unless he first binds the strong man? And then he will plunder his house" (Matt 12:29).

When Jesus expels demons from tormented people, it is visible evidence that the power of Satan is broken. Jesus is the stronger; he binds Satan and plunders the house the Devil had occupied. Jesus' own statement gives the key to understanding the larger significance of the exorcisms: "But if it is by the Spirit of God that I cast out demons, then the kingdom of God has come to you" (Matt 12:28).

The exorcisms of Jesus lose their meaning if they are disconnected from this larger context. Others could also perform exorcisms (both in the Jewish and the pagan environment of the first century), but these "ordinary" exorcisms only freed people from some of the concrete sufferings that came with possession. They were not lastingly transferred into a completely new reality. They would still live in the domain of the power of the demons and still had to fear them, try to appease them by some kind of cooperation with them or try to scare them off. The whole culture of antiquity was dominated by fear of demons and possession, and the ancient practice of exorcism supported and emphasised this fear rather than removed it.

The New Testament does not contain any explanation of why people become possessed. We should therefore avoid speculation as to the various reasons that may lie behind the New Testament stories of possession.

There is a large degree of continuity in the views of possession and exorcism in the Gospels, the early church as it is portrayed in Acts and in the ancient church. Central elements include: (1) the Devil and demons exist as evil, spiritual beings; (2) the connection between idolatry, paganism and possession; (3) Jesus Christ is the conqueror of the demons and shows his power in Christian exorcism and (4) the exorcisms are often situated in missionary situations where the gospel has not yet been preached.

Medicine

In 1 Timothy 5:23, Timothy is admonished to take a little wine for his stomach's sake on account of his frequent illness. The context, which is concerned with Timothy's health, makes clear that the wine is being prescribed here as a medicinal aid. Thus, while perhaps representing only a small strand in New Testament thought, the use of medicine as a response to infirmity cannot be ignored.

Evangelisation and Spiritual Conflict

In this section we will draw attention to the more general biblical view on the relation between evangelisation and spiritual conflict.

Signs and Wonders

The New Testament is very clear about the fact that *signs, miracles and wonders* are very much part of the church's proclamation of the gospel. Evidence for this is found in all the Gospels, in Acts and the Pauline literature (eg, Rom 15:18-19; 2 Cor 12:12; Gal 3:5; 1 Thess 1:5; Heb 2:4; 6:5). Thus, while there may be room for some disagreement on the issue of spiritual conflict, those who are committed to the task of world evangelisation should have an appreciation of and a place for signs and wonders as part of the gospel proclamation.

The Kingdom of God

There is a very strong emphasis in the first three Gospels on the *kingdom of God.* They are consistent in affirming that the kingdom is present and yet, has a future dimension. One of the ways in which the presence of the kingdom is demonstrated is through the exorcisms of Jesus (Matt 12:28; Luke 11:20), showing that part of the proclamation of the gospel involves conflict between God and the emissaries for good and the Devil and his forces (Luke 10:18-19; see also Acts 10:38).

The New Testament also underscores the ongoing conflict between God and the Devil. It is therefore not inappropriate to describe the Christian life as one engaged in spiritual conflict or spiritual warfare (see also Eph 6:11-17). Yet, it is also clear that this conflict is no dualistic struggle between two equal powers, but between an all-powerful God and less powerful forces in rebellion against the Lord.

Simplistic Equations

Despite the fact that Jesus and the disciples are engaged in a spiritual struggle, one cannot always assume that the Devil stands behind a given infirmity or affliction. *Simplistic equations* that always see a relation between illness or adversity and the Devil confuse the issue by ruling out of hand God's role and purpose in some events, while demonising infirmities that the New Testament may treat in a neutral fashion.

Similarly, a preoccupation with a paradigm of spiritual warfare in world evangelisation may obscure God's role and purposes in evangelising the nations or mistake neutral or natural events as Satan's attacks. It is clear from the Scriptures that the Devil and demons oppose the mission of the church; a reality that should never be ignored or underestimated. Yet, it is at the same time apparent that God may cause providential delays or struggles in world evangelisation for the sake of our Lord's greater plan (see eg, Acts 8:1-4; 16:6-10). It is possible that the church may misinterpret such delays or struggles owing to a preoccupation with spiritual warfare.

The Diversity of the New Testament Witness

We also need to be aware of the *diversity* in the New Testament witness. The kingdom of God paradigm, which is so dominant in the synoptic Gospels, is nearly absent in other New Testament writings. For example, John's gospel does not tell of any exorcism, and the only one who is accused of having a demon is Jesus (7:20; 8:48, 52; 10:20). We do not suggest that there is no cosmic struggle in the Johannine writings, but rather that there is some degree of diversity (not contradiction) among the New Testament writers. Therefore, an evangelistic strategy that focuses solely on one paradigm of spiritual conflict may be a less than holistic biblical approach to the mission of the church.

The Work of the Holy Spirit

The main biblical account of the evangelistic work of the early church, the Book of Acts, is literally full of examples of how God, through the *Holy Spirit*, is integrally involved in the mission of the church. God's activities include, among other things, empowering for witness (1:8), enabling Spirit-filled sermons (2; 4:8; 13:9), giving specific directions (8:29; 10:19; 11:12), calling certain people to mission (13:1-4), solving difficult theological issues (15:28), restraining from preaching in certain areas (16:6-7) and warning of dangers ahead (20:23; 21:4,11). From this it should be clear that part of the missionary task is to pay careful attention to what the Spirit is and is not saying with regard to the expansion of the kingdom. This underscores the need for an absolute reliance on the Spirit, not only to empower the mission, but also to direct it. An overemphasis on the spiritual warfare paradigm for evangelisation might, oddly enough, result in less of a reliance on the Holy Spirit by having room for only one aspect of the Spirit's ministry: the power encounter.

Territorial Spirits

With regard to the current issue of *territorial spirits* (see also section 8), the Old Testament can speak of spirits and/or angels in several ways. Reference is sometimes made to spirits who happen to be located in certain geographical areas, but who do not appear to have control over their places of abode. Specific mention is made of demons located in deserts (Lev 17:7; Isa 13:21; 34:14, cp Matt 12:43). In some texts, the gods are tied to specific geographical locations (1 Kings 20:23; 2 Kings 18:33, 35). The gods are sometimes identified with demons (Deut 32:8-17).

Certain Old Testament texts describe spirits and angels that are connected to specific nations (Dan 10:13,19-20). However, there are no hints that believers are to concern themselves with such spirits. The believer's role in the case of Daniel is largely defined as that of an observer of God's accomplishments on the broad screen of history. What is perhaps as significant is that there is no evidence in the New Testament that a concern about territorial spirits ever figured in the missionary strategy of the early Christians. Even when it is clear that Satan has hindered Paul from coming to Thessalonica (1 Thess 2:18), he does not engage in or advocate coming against Satan in spiritual warfare.

Demonic Influence on Believers

With regard to the question of demonic influence on believers, there appears on the one hand to be no direct biblical evidence that Christians may be controlled or possessed by a demon. On the other hand, it is clear that there is at least some precedent for the affliction of a believer by a demon. The role of the Devil and/or demons in temptation, deception, persecution and accusation of believers is amply documented.

Conclusion

We have in this section listened to the biblical testimony relating to some of the serious questions that are before us. We should, however, be aware that while listening to the biblical text is the most important part of the theological task, the hermeneutical method found in Acts 15 reveals that the early church not only had a place for the text in their interpretive activity, but also a very real appreciation for the activity of the Holy Spirit, as well as an appreciation for the role of the believing community in the interpretive process.

2. Spiritual Conflict in the History of the Church

In two papers on church history, Dr Oskar Skarsaune and Dr Tormod Engelsviken focused attention on the church's experience and views with regard to spiritual conflict, with particular reference to the question of possession and exorcism of evil spirits. Dr Skarsaune dealt mostly with the patristic period, while Dr Engelsviken followed the topic to contemporary times. Especially with regard to spiritual conflict, today's Christians may draw on a rich heritage of church history that stretches far back and beyond the influence of the post-Enlightenment rationalistic scientific paradigm.

The Ancient Church

Based on extensive textual evidence drawn from church fathers such as Tertullian, Justin Martyr, Theophilus of Antioch, Origen and Athanasius, it is possible to show that a particular set of thought was consistent throughout the ancient church. Several elements may be noted.

First is the conviction that the gods of the Gentiles are demons. The roots of this conception lie in the Old Testament. These gods exist, but they are not God (cf Deut 32:17). Gentiles relate to real powers in their cult, but these powers are demonic. "For all the gods of the peoples are idols" (Psalm 96:5, LXX) is frequently quoted by the church fathers.

Second is the idea that when people worship these demons in the pagan cult they risk possession. Possession is a phenomenon of paganism; it is connected with pagan worship. Possession does not occur, according to the church fathers, in the church among baptised people.

With regard to the question of the possibility of possession of Christians in the ancient church, two observations are important. The first concerns the use of a *pre-baptismal exorcism*. Already in the church order of Hippolytus (ca 210 AD), there exists a broadly developed set of pre-baptismal exorcisms:

> "From the day that they (who are to be baptised) are elected, let there be laying on of hands with exorcism every day. When the day of baptism approaches, let the bishop perform exorcism on each one of them, so that he may be certain that the baptized are clean. But if there is anybody who is not clean, he should be set aside because he did not hear the instruction with faith. For the alien spirit remained with him" (*Apostolic Tradition, 20,3*).

It seems as if the pre-baptismal exorcism is meant diagnostically to reveal and heal *possible* possession in the baptisands. There is also reason to believe that a preventive effect is ascribed to exorcism. Exorcistic prayers often also include a phrase that stops the spirit from future entrance into the person for whom the prayer is said. It may also be important that exorcisms take place before baptism because baptism is understood as a seal, a protective wall against possession, and it is imperative that the enemy be outside the city at the moment the wall is built. Pre-baptismal exorcism is still part of the baptismal ritual in some churches.

As concerns the question of possession among the baptised, the ancient church placed possession in pagan contexts. Where Christ rules, his power is at work so that demons must flee. May Christians nevertheless be possessed? Yes, according to the church fathers, but only if they actively seek the domains of the demons' power. Tertullian tells about a Christian woman who went to the theatre, where people slaughtered and maimed each other as entertainment for the masses, and came away possessed.

Third, as far as the setting or context of possession and exorcism in the ancient church is concerned, the literature and preaching about it were most often aimed at people outside the church. The great mass of evidence in the sources appears in apologetic and missionary literature. Exorcism, it appears, occurs primarily at the border between church and paganism; it is a missionary phenomenon. But this is where the importance is seen: exorcism is a sign that demonstrates that Christ has conquered Satan and his hosts. It is obvious that Christian exorcisms made deep impressions on people in antiquity. They were taken as proof of the resurrection of Jesus Christ because only a living Lord could exercise authority over demonic powers.

Finally, the ancient church was also of the conviction that Christian exorcism was totally efficient. There was no demon that did not bow to the name of Jesus. Several testimonies, both from Christian and pagan authors, confirm that Christians were recognised as effective exorcists. Besides the efficiency of Christian exorcism, people in antiquity were also struck by the fact that all Christians could do it, and that they did it without the usual complicated incantation techniques.

If we look at healing and exorcism as confirming signs that accompany preaching, it may look as if the ancient church placed more emphasis on exorcisms than on miraculous healings. The reason for this is not difficult to grasp: Christians were not alone in doing and experiencing miracles; the demons also performed them. Exorcism, however, functions as a "miracle of confrontation," where the demons are forced by the power of Jesus to openly admit who Jesus is and recognise that he is their superior. This may be the main reason for the great significance ascribed to exorcism in the missionary literature of the ancient church.

The Middle Ages

The development of the views and practices of the church during the Middle Ages, the Reformation and early post-Reformation times, with regard to the demonic and especially the question of possession and exorcism, is marked both by continuity and discontinuity in relation to the ancient church.

We have seen that a major view in the ancient church was to regard the gods of the Gentiles as demons masquerading as gods. The church looked upon the demons as "middle beings" between God and humans. They were created but did not have a physical body. The Devil was generally seen as having been created before humans as one of the angels, but had fallen due to the sin of pride. It was also assumed that it was possible for people to have contact both with angels and fallen angels.

Especially through the writings of the church father, Augustine, in the early fifth century, the understanding of the ancient church was communicated to the theologians of the Middle Ages. He held that the demons were both similar to God (eg, immortal) and to human beings (as created, moral beings), but qualitatively inferior to humans in that they were incapable of doing good. In the works of medieval theologians, the doctrine of angels and demons is dealt with in the framework of the doctrine of creation.

During the Middle Ages, however, popular religious ideas drawn from non-Christian sources influenced ordinary people's views of Satan and the demons. Pagan notions of different subterranean beings and other mythological figures were often mixed with the biblical concepts. The result was often a perversion of the biblical understanding. Grotesque images of the Devil with horn and hoofs often dominated popular imagination. Some of these images and ideas have been preserved with remarkable strength up until our own time, and have been used as an excuse to discard belief in the existence of the Devil altogether. One important reason why the church in the West today has great difficulties in communicating the biblical understanding of the Devil and demons is the fact that most non-Christians (rightfully) reject the associated non-Christian ideas.

Compared to the ancient church, the number of exorcisms and their missionary significance seems to have diminished during the Middle Ages. However, the Christianisation of the peoples of Northern and Eastern Europe again raised the question of the relation between Christ and the pagan gods. Historians of the Middle Ages speak about the significance of the "power encounter" for the Christianisation of the new tribes. The missionaries were not afraid of confronting paganism as when Boniface, the apostle of the Germans, in the eighth century chopped down a holy oak in Geismar, or when the St Olav, a not so saintly king, in the eleventh century struck down an idol in Norway. The leader of the pagan cult drew the following conclusion: "We have suffered great damage to our god. But since he was unable to help us, we will now believe in the god that you believe in." Then all of them received the Christian faith.

It is often assumed that the *pagan* influence in the newly converted tribes contributed to a change in the popular Christian view of demonic influence, and created a close association, almost identification, of some humans with demons. An expression of this was the idea of a common flight of witches and demons. It is important to note, however, this view was rejected by the official church. These thoughts, towards the end of the Middle Ages in the fifteenth century and the pre-Enlightenment era of Europe, developed into the witch hysteria that led to the deplorable execution of tens of thousands accused as witches.

This *witch hunt* is often held against the church as an almost inevitable result of the church's doctrine of the Devil and demons, and many studies have been made of this very sad incident in the history of the Western church, both Protestant and Catholic. Some facts should, however, be emphasised to correct some errors in the popular opinion.

First, witch hunts in Europe did not belong in the Middle Ages, but in the Renaissance and the post-Reformation period. The main period in Europe is the time from about 1580 to 1680. Both before and after this one-hundred-years period, there were few witch-hunting campaigns.

Second, the typical "witch" was not a beautiful young woman. Indeed, most were old and roughly one-fifth were men.

Additionally, the court cases against them were not initiated by the church and were held before secular courts. The charges against the "witches" most often came from the local community, not from the ecclesiastical authorities. It often concerned marginal people in marginal areas (eg, the mountain areas in the Alps, Pyrenees and Norway), not in the central areas (eg, Rome or other major cities). Priests often played little or no role in the cases, but could sometimes be drawn upon as "spiritual experts."

Finally, the infamous inquisition in Spain played a surprising role in dampening the witch-hunting frenzy. The investigation and report of Spanish inquisitors often put an end to witchcraft accusations, revealing that the false charges were founded on superstition.

The reasons for witch hunts include a combination of social, economic and psychological factors, but the church also had a responsibility because during this period it accepted a "witch doctrine" that made the secular courts take the accusations seriously. The understanding of witchcraft was a combination of different ideas, many of them of non-Christian origins, eg, the concept of magic, the idea of an implicit or explicit covenant between humans and demons and a projection of fear and anxiety. The theological justification was expressed in the literary work *Malleus Maleficarum* (Witch Hammer) from 1487.

In perspective, we have to say that there is no Christian justification for violent persecution of so-called witches. There is also no necessary connection between a biblical understanding of the Devil and demons and this hysteria that gripped some areas of Europe during this time. Any church participation in this persecution must be deeply deplored. The sad experience of the church in Europe in this regard should stand as a warning against similar abuses at other times in other cultures.

The Lutheran Reformation

The Reformation in the sixteenth century did not significantly alter the worldview of the Middle Ages. Several works of the German reformer Martin Luther contain references to Satan and demons. But in this area, as well as others, he had a more biblical orientation than his Catholic predecessors.

According to Luther, human beings are, in their sinfulness, subject to the powers of the flesh, the world and the Devil. These powers of corruption are often mentioned together because they are "allies" in their efforts to lead people to damnation. Satan, the prince of this world, does his work primarily through human sinful nature. He seduces and tempts people to sin and keeps them in bondage to sin. A personal evil will is the origin of sin and it catches the will of individual people as well as that of the whole of humanity.

Luther's radical view of the reality of Satan had as its background his own spiritual struggle. "By the grace of God I have come to know a lot about Satan," Luther says. He takes Satan and evil more seriously than most of his contemporaries. Satan is the great adversary of Christ. According to Luther, the conflict between God and Satan runs through all of history, and it is impossible for human beings to be neutral. But it is not an equal battle in a dualistic sense. Satan can only work within the limits set by God's omnipotence. Satan has been defeated and he and his power will finally be destroyed by the return of Christ. Through the gospel, God rescues people from the power of Satan.

Luther understood the Lord's Prayer, and especially the prayer "Deliver us from evil," as directed against the Devil as well as to God. His famous hymn, "A Mighty Fortress is Our God," is a testimony to Luther's realistic conception of Satan as well as to his triumphant sense of victory in Christ.

Luther also holds on to a biblical realism as far as the demons are concerned. He maintained that one could and should drive the evil spirits out of the possessed by prayer.

We know of at least one case of possession from the time of the Reformation that clearly shows the attitude of the reformers. Johannes Bugenhagen, one of Luther's close co-workers, wrote a letter to the theologians in Wittenberg, Germany, among them Luther, where he describes his meeting with a possessed girl in Lübeck. The detailed description of this case corresponds wholly with other cases of possession known from history. Luther himself refers to the letter from Bugenhagen and accepts the possession as a fact.

The Lutheran confessional writings in the sixteenth century do not refer to possession or exorcism, but they express in many places the biblical and historical view of the Devil and the way to fight him and guard against him: The Word of God, the name of God and prayer drive him away.

The Post-Reformation Era

It is not possible here to describe the views and practices with regard to the Devil and the demonic in the whole of the Reformation and in all the later Protestant churches. One example from the post-Reformation period may be mentioned, namely the Danish-Norwegian Lutheran Church.

We have seen that exorcism in connection with baptism was kept in the church down through the centuries from the earliest time, without implying that all who were not baptised were possessed by evil spirits. As infant baptism became more common, exorcism became part of the baptismal ritual itself. In the Danish-Norwegian church, the formula "Depart [lit. Go out] you evil spirit, and give room for the Holy Spirit" was used until 1783 when it was removed after some controversy. The removal took place at the time of the Enlightenment. However, a *renunciation* of the Devil and all his works was retained in the baptismal liturgy prior to the confession of faith and it is still in use.

The Church Ritual of 1685 contains guidelines for the treatment of demonic possession. The pastor is not to assume that possession occurs often "for such examples are at the present time rare in Christendom", but neither should he think "that we now are totally free from these attacks by Satan". After a thorough investigation together with doctors and other pastors in order to ascertain whether it is a natural disease or whether the person is "bodily possessed by the Devil so that he rules and governs in the whole body and all its members, as well as in mind, reason and the attributes of the soul", the pastor may go on to pray for the possessed person.

At this point, it might have been possible to go on to present and discuss the forms and reasons for the post-Enlightenment theological rejection of the reality of a personal devil and the possibility of demonic possession. It would, however, take us far into Western intellectual history and necessitate a discussion of the modern Western rationalistic worldview. Suffice it here to state, that in contemporary Protestantism, the concepts of the Devil and demons are mostly used in a merely metaphorical sense. The general assumption by most people in the Western world, an assumption that also is reflected in the dominant theological works and dictionaries of our time, is that it is no longer possible to believe in the existence and influence of created spiritual beings, be it angels or demons (although people seem to be more inclined to believe in angels than demons), and that the Devil and the demons are mythological expressions of what is often called "transpersonal evil."

Although some modern theologians are aware that in evangelical and Pentecostal circles there is still a belief in a personal devil, and that exorcism is practiced, this is nevertheless not seen as a serious subject for most contemporary theological reflection. In the West, the post-Enlightenment rationalist rejection of the biblical worldview with regard to the Devil is still so pervasive that the biblical and historical presuppositions of this consultation are in conflict with the mainstream of contemporary Protestant thought.

Conclusion

It should be emphasised that the evangelical church will do well in listening to the historical experience of the universal church in its various traditions and learn from its mistakes and successes. Only as it evaluates history in light of the Scriptures and the experiences of the worldwide church today will it be able to find the right way forward.

3. A Systematic Theological View of Spiritual Conflict

Dr Hwa Yung wrote the major paper on a systematic, theological approach to spiritual conflict. Initially, he pointed out that even where theological texts have been produced in the non-Western world, as in recent years, much of the underlying assumptions and thought patterns in these have been conditioned by modernity and its mechanistic, naturalistic worldview learned from the West. Given these facts, up until the early 1980s, there have been very few books that wrestled seriously with the personal demonic dimension in the world. But the rise of the Pentecostal-charismatic renewal on the one hand and the New Age movement on the other, both in the West, together with the increasing growth and strength of non-Western Christianity, have forced the church to wrestle much more with a badly neglected area.

Worldview Issues

The question of worldview is of crucial importance in dealing with spiritual conflict. Increasingly, it is now recognised that the naturalistic and mechanistic worldview of modernity has now collapsed. But are the teachers and writers on spiritual warfare and related issues in danger of slipping back into an animistic worldview or adopting the worldview of New Age or of post-modernity? What constitutes a proper biblical understanding of demonic powers, the basics of which apply across space and time? The first question that we must address is what is normative and what is culturally conditioned.

One cannot simply dismiss the demonic as a cultural hangover from New Testament times. Whether demons are real or not must be judged on the basis of all evidence available. On this, both biblical revelation and the sum total of empirical evidence from all over the world point to the ontological reality of such beings, even if we are to set aside Jewish apocalyptic language and the specific terms for demons as being culturally conditioned. The only culture or worldview that has systematically denied it is that of modernity in the West. Even there, all have not accepted it. Beneath the surface level of modern Western societies, there are still multiple folk religious practices and beliefs, including beliefs in spiritual beings, magic, astrology, spiritualism and other occult practices. Increasingly, these practices have become more open and popular, especially within the new religious movements.

Elements of Christian Demonology

A Christian doctrine of demonic powers based on the Bible should include a number of crucial elements.

Satan and Demons Are Real, Personal, Spiritual Beings

The Bible provides no answer as to the origin of Satan and demons. Some have speculated that Isaiah 14 and Ezekiel 28 allude to Satan's origin and fall. But there remain uncertainties as to the actual meaning of these passages. It would therefore be wise not to be dogmatic about this. What is almost certain is that Satan and his minions are angelic beings created by God who subsequently rebelled against God.

Numerous references to fallen angels, demons and evil spirits are found in both Testaments. In the New Testament, there are numerous accounts of encounters of Jesus and his disciples with demonic powers in both the Gospels and Acts. This evidence alone, and the teachings of Jesus, asserts the reality of demonic powers.

Nevertheless, against the background of some recent writings on spiritual warfare, it is important also to note what Paul does not teach. Paul is silent on at least five areas: (1) an explanation of the angelic rebellion and fall, (2) the names of the angelic powers, (3) the order within the angelic hierarchy, (4) the activities of certain demons and how they are thwarted and (5) the territories ruled by evil spirits. Other biblical writers, as well as Jesus himself, are also largely silent on these. It would appear that the proper Christian approach is to avoid going beyond what Scripture teaches (cf Deut 29:29).

How Satan and His Demons Work

Satan and his hosts influence every level of human existence. Here we will restrict our attention to the most significant for spiritual conflict.

Sin and Temptation. The Bible emphasises that Satan and his minions are opposed to God's work in every way. They not only entice us through temptations of all kinds, but also fully exploit our human propensity to sin through the weakness of our flesh and our enslavement to sin apart from the power of the Holy Spirit.

Possession or Demonisation. There are several clear incidents involving possessed persons in the Gospels and Acts. The deliverance of these persons through the authority of Jesus Christ has been replicated countless times through the ministry of Christians down the ages. Moreover, this continues to take place in the present, especially where the gospel regularly encounters those who come from a background of non-Christian religious practices, occult involvement or addictions to sins of all kinds.

Illnesses. Many Christians are not in the habit of thinking of illnesses as having possible demonic origins. Yet, the Bible contains a number of clear references to this and even today this has been the experience of many who have been involved in healing ministry.

Nature. Within a holistic worldview, both the work of God and the angels on the one hand and demonic powers on the other must be understood to impact not just the spiritual realm but rather the whole of life, including nature. Occult influences on nature are commonly known in cultures where non-Christian religions and occult practices flourish.

Society and State. The powers influence society and state first and foremost through individuals, and secondly, through the Pauline concepts of "world" and "this age" which would correspond closely to our present-day understanding of structural evil.

The Occult. This is the realm where humans have sometimes been given to think that they are in a position to manipulate the powers of darkness for their own advantage. But oftentimes, they discover too late who the real masters are. In fact, in mediumistic practices, those involved often have little choice in the matter because they are eventually "possessed" and co-opted by the spirits to do their bidding.

Non-Christian Religions. It has to be firmly stated that non-Christian religions do contain some things that are true, right and noble. They also contain, however, demonic elements, often linked in different ways to occult practices. For example, priests in Buddhist and Hindu temples, and Muslim Sufi leaders are often involved in such practices. Similar examples are found in the Bible.

Christus Victor and the Defeat of Satan

Given the above reality, how does the Christian respond to the powers of darkness? The Bible's answer is clear: Christ has decisively defeated Satan at the Cross; he is the conqueror, *Christus Victor*.

Evangelical theology has tended to interpret the Cross through the penal substitution model, and rightly so. However, this has often been done in such a way as to imply that that model exhausts the meaning of the Cross. While it needs to be emphasised that penal substitution is the basic model for understanding the Cross, other models can supplement its meaning. In particular, in dealing with demonic powers, the Christus Victor model, which stresses Christ's victory over sin, Satan and death, needs to be emphasised. Indeed, the victory of Christ logically flows out of his substitutionary atonement for sinful humanity on the Cross. Because the penalty for sin has been paid and judgment averted, sin, Satan and death no longer have any hold over redeemed humanity (Col 2:13-15). Christians are, therefore, now in a position to appropriate the authority of Christ (Luke 9:1; Matt 28:18) and to stand in the victory that we have in him (Eph 6:11,13).

The War Continues until Christ Returns

God, in his sovereignty, has not yet completely destroyed Satan and his host. They remain extremely dangerous and potent. The Christian is called to be always on the lookout. Paul reminds us that the war is still on (Eph 6:10-18), and we have defensive as well as offensive roles to play.

The thrust of biblical teaching on how the war against Satan and his host can be won is seen in Revelation 12:11, which was written in the context of intense persecution and, one may surmise, ferocious Satanic attack. Yet, the writer does not speak anywhere of techniques that will ensure victory. Rather, Christians are called to overcome the powers of darkness by standing on the victory won by "the blood of the Lamb," through the faithful "word of their testimony" and by learning not to "cling to life even in the face of death." Thus, the emphasis is on standing on the victory of Christ, faithful witness, willingness to suffer even unto death and diligent trusting prayer.

Does Satan Have Dominion Over the World?

Another issue that needs some consensus concerns Satan's claim that he has authority over "all the kingdoms of the earth" (Luke 4:5-6). He further claims "their glory and all this authority . . . has been given over to me, and I can give it to anyone I please." Does he indeed have such authority? If he does, how was it given to him?

On the first question, it has been argued that Satan is merely lying. After all, he is "a liar and the father of lies" (John 8:44). Moreover, if it is true that Satan has authority over the world, surely that contradicts the belief in God's sovereignty over the world. But in response to this, two things may be said.

First, Satan's claim to have authority is reinforced by Jesus' references to him as "the ruler of this world" (John 12:31; 14:30; and 16:11), and by Paul as the "god of this world" (2 Cor 4:4) and "the ruler of the power of the air" (Eph 2:2).

Second, it is clear that the Bible uses the term *world* in at least two ways; first, the world which God created, and second, human society in rebellion against God. It would appear that in the references above made by Jesus and Paul, *world* or *age* is used in the second sense. In that sense, Satan is indeed "the ruler of this world". Satan may be exaggerating his powers in making the claim that he has authority over "all the kingdoms of the earth" because God remains sovereign over his creation. But nevertheless, it appears that he does rule over a limited sphere, that of the *world* of humankind in rebellion against God, with its pride and arrogance, disordered priorities and false values, disobedient human hearts and evil socio-political structures.

If this is the case, then how was Satan given that authority? The answer is that we, as humans, through our fall gave Satan that authority over our lives and our communities. This would sound terribly glib, except for the fact that Paul reminds us that it was because "sin came into the world through one man, and death came through sin, and so death spread to all, because all have sinned", and that "just as one man's trespass led to condemnation for all" (Rom 5:12, 18; cp also Rom 1:21-32). Further, it was this that has led to our enslavement to sin (Rom 7:7-25). It must be admitted that nowhere does the Bible explicitly teach that it was our sin that gave Satan authority over us and the *world*. But Christian theology has always linked the tyranny of sin, death and Satan over human life together. Thus, it would appear correct to conclude that it is indeed human sin that gave Satan authority over us.

This would also tie in with what was said earlier about the Cross. Penal substitution is the basic model for the atonement. But, it must be complemented by the Christus Victor model. The latter flows from the former. Penal substitution frees us from sin and its condemnation. Once that has been dealt with, we are freed from bondage to sin, death and Satan and can now share in Christ's victory through his death over all three. Thus the logic flows as follows: it was our sin that gave the Devil authority over our lives in the first place; but once Christ has dealt with that, we can have victory over Satan!

Theology from Above or Below?

The final question we need to briefly look at is how we are to approach the formulation of a more comprehensive biblical-based demonology. Indeed, the question is not whether it should be from above, that is starting from the Bible, or below, beginning with empirical evidence. As in all of theology, our understanding of God is derived from revelation, and then further clarified and explicated through our experiences.

The issues at hand are two-fold. First, we need a more careful study of Scripture, which will allow us to transcend the biases of our own limited worldviews. That will give us a clearer understanding of what the Bible teaches about the powers of darkness. Second, we need to draw together the vast experiences of Christians throughout history and from different cultures, and carefully analyse these in light of what Scripture teaches. Much of what has been written in recent years on spiritual warfare has an anecdotal character. It constitutes a vast body of empirical data that is potentially helpful, and therefore should not be jettisoned by those who have difficulties with some of these writings. How they are to be interpreted is the important point. Careful attention to these two fundamental issues can only help to advance the gospel against the kingdom of darkness.

4. Spiritual Conflict Today: Case Histories

The experiences of spiritual conflict in different contexts vary to a great extent, but they also have much in common. Through listening to voices from different parts of the world, we noticed significant differences in experience and interpretation. We sought to hear how spiritual conflict is actually perceived and practised around the world. These stories, at times in harmony and at times out of harmony, are the contexts in which the church has to speak and minister. In the presentation of these case studies, we have kept the first person voice as much as possible.

East Asia

Dr Hwa Yung from Malaysia shared from his experience of the realities of the spirit realm in East Asian life. He maintained that even seemingly secularised people are religious. Religion is often intertwined with the occult as, for example, temple practices are often linked to the occult through mediumistic practices relating to ancestral spirits. Some temples are especially known for their powerful, protective charms and amulets. Mediums are common and spirit possession happens repeatedly. There is, overall, a tremendous fear of spirits.

Sometimes, a deity in a local temple adopts children. In such cases, it often takes a long time for them to become Christians. A cleansing process is necessary in which their adoption has to be renounced. Possession may occur even among Christians, especially when their parents have been mediums. In these cases a process of cleansing is needed.

Three major conclusions can be drawn, based on observations of the situation in East Asia:

1. There is a close relation between evangelistic breakthroughs and power encounters. In every place where the gospel advances, there are real power encounters. The result is often rapid growth.

2. Indigenous church movements emphasise the power of the Holy Spirit and Pentecostal-charismatic practices. It seems that when Christians read the Bible for themselves and practise what they read, Pentecostal traits are manifested.

3. With regard to the question of whether Christians may be possessed, the Asian experience tells us when Christians come to Christ out of a non-Christian environment, cleansing must take place; otherwise, demonic powers invariably have a hold on them.

India

An Indian case history was presented by the Reverend V. Ezekiah Francis. He shared the following two experiences of spiritual conflict.

Tamil Nadu

A city in Tamil Nadu was known for prostitution and sexual perversion. Several attempts to conduct evangelistic meetings met with stiff resistance. The attendance at such meetings was negligible. Therefore, we waited upon the Lord, wanting to know what should be done. The Lord showed us that the entire place was under demonic control. Then, the Holy Spirit led us to bind the strong man first. We arranged for chain prayer with fasting. When this was done, the answer came to us and there was a large gathering of more than 5,000 people.

Muscat

Once when I was ministering in Muscat, a lady came to me for prayer. She had been suffering from severe headaches for several years. No medical treatment helped. After praying for her, I counselled her to spend more time with the Word of God and in the presence of the Lord.

The moment I said this, she broke down and said that the severity of her headache increased. I then inquired about her past. She hailed from a Hindu background. Her parents were idol worshippers and she too had participated in all religious functions. She carried 'Kavadi' (a decorated stand with an idol) on her shoulders. The headaches started then.

It was clear that the spirit behind that idol was tormenting her. I took authority in the name of Jesus, commanded the Devil to release its hold and go out of that lady. Within minutes, she started vomiting. That was the end of the headaches.

Ethiopia

The Reverend Amsalu Tadesse Geleta, a pastor from the Ethiopian Evangelical Church Mekane Yesus (EECMY), prepared a case study on exorcism in the Ethiopian context.

He noted that the daily experience of Christians in Ethiopia is that Christ is stronger than Satan. Most prayer meetings, and also individual prayers, include rebuking of evil spirits. Prayers are offered for protection and songs of worship and thanksgiving are sung because God has overcome the power of darkness.

Causes of Possession

Personal involvement in the occult, eg, *Qalicha* or so-called *zar* worship, is one of the major causes of possession. Often, the mediumistic powers of *Qalichas* and traditional cults can be traced back over some generations in one family. Most possessed people who come to the church for help have been involved in occult rituals. The reason is often a vow that the possessed has taken to achieve some advantage or help in a critical situation. Such a vow may involve a sacrifice to the spirits or the dedication of some pieces of property, eg, rings, pots and sticks.

Naqamte

It was around six o'clock in the evening. An evangelist of Naqamte congregation (EECMY Central Synod) and I were at the main entrance of the church compound. A group of about ten people brought a man chained to a Land Rover pickup. While they were struggling to hold him down, we asked what had happened.

They told us that something was wrong with him and no one could hold him, even with ropes. We brought him to the church to see if we could get help. There was no one in the church to pray for the man. We took courage to do so. We rebuked the evil spirit and told him to be quiet, and then ordered the people to untie his ropes. They told us the man could escape. We assured them he would not. We then ordered the demoniac to walk into the church.

We shared the gospel with those who brought the man. All of them were non-Christian neighbours who had come to assist his wife in bringing him to the church. We preached the victorious Christ, not only over the evil spirit, but also over the sins of the people.

Then we told the evil spirit to reveal himself, who he was and why he had possessed the man. The spirit claimed that it was the spirit of the serpent (*hafura Jawe*), and *dache* (literally "beneath" in the Oromo language). The spirits said that they had attacked him because he had disturbed them while they had a coffee ceremony in the middle of the day. In addition, the spirits said the person had no cover or protection and was vulnerable to their attack. Afterwards, he sinned continuously doing all the spirits urged him to do. Their aim was to kill him as an offering.

Those who had brought the person were curiously observing what we did. We were all praying and praising God. The absence of any devices, except the use of the name of Jesus, made a special impact on the spectators. We rebuked the spirits one by one until the last spirit left, affirming that it was leaving.

The person stayed reclined for about five minutes. Then he stood up wondering how he had come there. He realised he was in the church. He went home carrying the rope with which he was tied when he came. He came tied and went home free. The event was one of practical evangelisation for the others present.

West Africa

Dr Yusufu Turaki from Nigeria presented a comprehensive look at African traditional religious systems as a basis for understanding spiritual conflict in an African setting. His case study presentation began with these challenges to Christianity:

1. Non-Christian religions and worldviews are currently bombarding the churches and Christians with the non-Christian gospel. These are invading our homes and private lives through society and culture, especially through the media presentations that surround us.

2. Political religion and political culture, notably as seen in Islam in Nigeria, is a great threat to the church.

3. The traditional African worldview is permeated with the reality of the spirit realm and spiritual phenomena. The Bible portrays a similar emphasis on spiritual phenomena. But, in the church in Nigeria there is a theology that blocks the church in Africa from seeing what is in African Tradition Religions (ATRs), and what is in Scripture.

How are we to address African Christianity? Some say we need intense African cultural studies, and some say all we need is the Bible. Turaki proposed that we need both so that the biblical worldview can address the African worldview.

The foundational religious beliefs in ATRs include beliefs in impersonal mystical powers, spirit beings, many deities/gods in a hierarchy and in the Supreme Being. These beliefs have corresponding religious practices, including establishing links with spiritual powers, means of exercising spiritual control (eg, incantations, symbols, magic, charms, amulets, fetishes or juju, witchcraft, sorcery and divination), names relating to spiritual powers, rituals that will restore spiritual powers and means of spiritual and mystical communication (usually through specialists such as diviners, mediums and sorcerers).

What is the significance of the traditional African worldview? The gospel confronted Africans at the level of religious beliefs. But Africans have more religious practices than beliefs, so missionaries introduced new religious practices and social institutions that host both religious beliefs and practices. Additionally, the colonial leaders confronted the Africans at these levels and displaced the traditions. As a result, some Africans broke away to form independent churches that emphasised the African worldview rather than the Western one.

Eventually, there resulted an African re-evangelisation of Western Christianity as African intellectuals critiqued Western Christianity. This critique came from a rational African cultural perspective, resulting in a rational African-culture Christianity — once again leaving out the spirit realm.

Today, however, the supernatural perspective has experienced resurgence. One result is the accusation of African leaders as being witches because their children died off. Thus, while we may say Africa is 'modernised' or 'Christianised', the real worldview has been largely unchanged. Even though hybrid institutions that borrow from both the West and Africa have replaced traditional social and religious institutions, the concepts of the traditional institutions still live on in the worldview of the people.

The younger generation in particular has recovered the spiritual (both in the church and traditional settings), but has rejected the rational approach of the older generation of Christians. When youth come to Christ, they bring into the church traditional meanings. Thus, terms such as the 'blood of Christ' are not viewed rationally, but in terms of traditional religious (magical) perspectives. They apply this worldview to all that they see in the church.

The older churches (those over 100 years old) are generally not experiencing these spiritual phenomena, though the younger churches are. Among them, though, such phenomena are re-interpreted in light of traditional magical thinking and moving in multiple spiritual directions (eg, a prosperity approach to the gospel parallel to acquiring power in traditional religion). In Nigeria, for example, New Age religions have flourished by converting the younger generation. They have done so by playing on the African concept of the spiritual phenomena.

Western Europe

Ole Skerbæk Madsen is a pastor in the Lutheran Church in Denmark that comprises about 90% of the population. He works primarily among "New Age" spiritual seekers. In 1995, he started a work called "In the Master's Light." At the consultation, he shared the background and the methods of this ministry.

Spiritual Conflict Among European New Agers

The most important spiritual conflict with New Age has to do with *teachings* that contradict the saving truths of God's self-revelation in Jesus Christ the Son and the Holy Spirit — in creation, in the history of salvation and in the Bible. Some of the religious *practices* are also dubious from a Christian point of view. What are the sources of channelled messages? What are the energies or entities behind the symbols of tarot and astrology? In my practice as a pastor, I have met several people who mentally and spiritually were deeply hurt through such practices and left in confusion because of the New Age doctrines. Some had to be helped through inner healing or deliverance, many through an act of confirmation and renewed commitment to their baptismal covenant (most people in Denmark are baptised as infants in the Lutheran Church). In short, they had to receive Jesus in their hearts and turn to God as revealed in Jesus Christ.

As Christians, we are often involved in a spiritual conflict with modern seekers and New Age. The conflict is no doubt a fact, but the fear of demons and the fear of being demonised through contact with the new spirituality and the milieu of seekers is perhaps the greatest danger for us. One of the strategies of the Enemy is to blind our spiritual and mental faculties from recognising the dedication to the quest for meaning, wholeness and fulfilment in our fellow human beings. We must not be so preoccupied with our resentment against many of their wrong or strange practices and their false doctrines that we forget they are sincere seekers, loved by God and potential disciples of Jesus and worshippers of the true God — if they meet the love of God in Jesus Christ and in the power of the Holy Spirit. They need to meet Jesus Christ *first* through love and care that will help them interpret their experiences in a different way.

In the spiritual conflict in the milieu of seekers, our main strategy is not to discuss right doctrines, opposing all that we conceive of as dangerous, false or even demonic. This would only estrange us from those to whom we would like to present the gospel and leave them stuck in their criticism of the church. Our strategy is a positive one: we have to be among the seekers as disciples of our Master and have within us the spirit of disciples. It is this dynamic love-faith relation between the Master and the disciples that will be the authentic answer to the quest of the modern spiritual seekers.

Another factor that attracts seekers is the charismatic dimension of the disciples as the body of Christ. The gifts of the Spirit are the authentic means of inspiration and healing. Charismatic fellowships and churches may become new spiritual centres because of the presence of the Master and because the power of the Holy Spirit which helps the seeker to taste the true new age — that is the kingdom of God.

In the Master's Light

In the summer of 1994, Jesus told me to start some spiritual meetings in the New Age milieu under the title "*In the Master's Light.*" The services started in May 1995. In them, we recognise the quest of New Agers and share many of their values, such as their reaction to materialism and self-interest. We respect their genuine quest for spiritual values in a materialistic age, but we are very specific in expressing that among all the spiritual masters in the seekers' sphere, Jesus is our *only* Master. We try to meet the longing to learn spiritual values with teachings inspired by the Holy Spirit.

We expect the Holy Spirit to inspire preaching and to give prophecy and revelation. When Jesus spoke to me on *In the Master's Light,* he promised a prophetic message for each meeting. We call these messages "inspirations" or "the direct communication of the Master." We try to meet the longing for wholeness and healing by inviting those present for the healing of their heart. We avoid adversarial arguments in speaking with those present, but rather try to share experiences. We witness that the testimony of a disciple of Jesus is a seed of truth. In order to plant such seeds of truth, we first have to listen to the other people, their experiences, beliefs, values and needs. We try to use the seekers' language and forms to express our own spirituality and walk with the Master.

We have learned not to press seekers into conformity with ourselves. We do not start by correcting their opinions, but we invite them to meet the Master and to taste the goodness and loving kindness of our Lord and Saviour, Jesus Christ. When they begin reorienting their lives around their experience of Jesus, we accept them as fellow disciples. The more they focus on the Master, the more we trust them to correct what is not in accordance with the Master's teachings and the presence of the Holy Spirit in their lives.

Today, we have *In the Master's Light* in eight places in Denmark. In 1999, we prayed with more than 1,500 seekers for the healing of their heart in their relation to God, to their own inner being and to the surrounding world. We have had retreats and workshops and have been present at New Age exhibitions. We have also been invited to share our faith in New Age magazines, radio programmes and societies. Many New Agers now come regularly for worship and pastoral care.

Brazil

Dr Neuza Itioka, a female teacher and "prayer warrior" in Brazil, shared several stories of spiritual conflict in Brazil. This is but one of them.

Iemanja Followers

It was December 31, New Year's Eve. For many Brazilians, this is the night for bringing in the New Year. But it is also a night in which Iemanja, the spirit of the waters, brought over from Africa, is invoked. A group of young people from an evangelical church decided to go to the beach for evangelism. They filled up a bus and went down the mountain to the sea. On this date, between 1 and 1.5 million people go down to the beach to honour Iemanja, offering perfume, champagne, jewellery, flowers and food to the spirit of the waters in exchange for benefits in the areas of health, love and material prosperity.

The young people had prayed, prepared themselves and even fasted, in order to be ready to face the difficult cases of evangelism that might arise. When they arrived at the beach, they parked the bus near the statue of Iemanja, which was already duly ornamented for her celebration.

Nearby, they saw a woman swirling in the sand. They understood she was invoking the spiritual entities to be incorporated in her. Stopping at that place, they began to pray quietly, forbidding the demons, as they understood them to be, to enter her body. After a while the woman, whose eyes had been closed, stopped swirling, opened her eyes and said, "What's going on here? I am invoking the entities and they don't come?" The young people answered, "Good evening. We are here, and we are forbidding them to come to you, in the name of Jesus." She protested, "But I'm invoking them in the name of Jesus, too." Thus, they began to share their faith, telling her about Jesus, the Son of the Almighty God, who was not just any Jesus, but Jesus, Lord of the Universe, who came in flesh and blood. They told her about God's great love. This encounter led the woman to kneel down in the sand and open her heart to receive the Lord Jesus. This new convert revealed that she was a Mother of Saints, a priestess in Umbanda, one of the Brazilian religions, and she asked, "Please, come to my *terreiro* (spiritist temple) to tell my people about this wonderful Jesus."

The young people, excited about what was happening, prayed, fasted and then went to preach to those people who had gathered together to invoke African gods that had been mixed with Catholic saints and other spiritist practices. There were, as could be expected, struggles and reactions, but that *terreiro* was transformed into a Baptist congregation. The gospel was powerful for the transformation and conversion of an Umbanda priestess and the result of this transformation was that all of these people were brought to Jesus Christ.

North America

Dr Charles Kraft has extensive experience in dealing with evil spirits, what he calls "rats." He shared the following about his own ministry.

Jesus spent a good bit of his time and energy healing and casting out demons. Most of us find, however, that our record for healing is not as good as Jesus' and that simply commanding demons out, as the Gospels show Jesus doing, is often not sufficient to free people. There are, therefore, a variety of styles extant among those of us who are active in healing and deliverance ministries. My own focus tends to be on inner-healing based ministries, which focus almost exclusively on dealing with emotional and/or spiritual "garbage" or, after dealing with the garbage, go on to tackle any demonic "rats" that might be attached to the garbage.

I look for demons (and usually find them) if the amount of garbage the person has been carrying seems to indicate their presence. We have observed that the strength of demons is calibrated to the amount and kind of garbage in the client's life. Thus, if we do not want to have to fight with the demons, we find that the best thing to do is to use inner-healing techniques to deal with the garbage. We can then free the person from the demons later. With this approach, we almost never have any violence, vomiting or other disagreeable happenings.

By garbage, I mean such things as generational or contemporary dedications; curses, vows or pacts made with enemy spirits or gods; dedications to spirits or gods by persons in authority over the client or by the client himself; self-cursing; wallowing in negative emotions such as anger, unforgiveness, hatred, shame or the like; having death wishes or inviting spirits of death in via abortion, suicide attempts and so on; and inviting in spirits of homosexuality and the like.

We, who use my approach, assume that there may be a double cause underlying the person's problems: a human one (garbage) and a spirit one (demons). We find that if there are demons, we can assume there is a human cause (the garbage). If there is human garbage, though, there are not necessarily demons, especially if the amount of garbage is small. We recognise then, that the demons are a secondary problem, not the primary one. In order for them to be there, they must have legal rights given them by those who created the garbage.

5. Spiritual Conflict and Folk Religions

Suffering, misfortune and evil are part of all human life. How these are understood and explained varies, however, as do the methods used to alleviate the problems. The major world religions have addressed the matter in philosophical arguments, but for most people in the world these explanations fail to address the practical aspects of daily life. For these questions, answers are sought in the non-empirical realm of folk religion. In his paper Dr David G. Burnett argued that it is often the issues raised by folk religion that may be most relevant in spiritual conflict.

Folk Religion

The late nineteenth century saw the categorisation of religious traditions by Western scholars into Islam, Hinduism, Buddhism and so on. These religions of major civilisations were therefore considered "world religions." However, such categories create gaps, and into these gaps were gathered heaps of intransigent phenomena. The category "traditional religion" tends to be the catch phrase for all other religious expressions from whatever part of the world they may originate.

One may distinguish between three permeable bands: "philosophical world religion," "folk religion" and finally "traditional religion." The latter two bands are distinguished by whether or not the people acknowledge an allegiance to a world religion. The middle band or "folk religion" is usually a re-working of long-existing beliefs, but within the confession of the major religion.

These differences have also been seen as differences between "high" and "low" religion. High religions may be more philosophical in their explanation, whilst folk beliefs are based upon the existing worldview into which the teaching of the world religion is incorporated. In folk religion, people look for explanations and answers different from those offered by the more philosophical religion.

This model has become a popular concept among Christian missionaries because it gives a simple way of explaining the differences they have observed between philosophical and local aspects of major religious traditions. It is in the realm of folk belief that much of the discussion of spiritual conflict has its context.

Causes of Misfortune in Folk Religion

Why do bad things happen? Most societies perceive two common causes of evil: spiritual beings and people. It is important that these aspects always be seen as part of the wider culture and not as distinct elements. To fail to appreciate this means a failure to appreciate the underlying fears and beliefs that are inherent within the society as a whole.

Spiritual Beings

Although a belief in a Supreme Being, or "High God" who is the creator, is common to most traditional religions, he is usually considered distant and unconcerned with human affairs. It is the lesser gods and spirits that are bound up with human experience. They are neither totally good nor totally evil, and they may range from powerful spirits, which must be treated with respect, to relatively insignificant spirits of the forest, field or water who may merely cause a nuisance. Often, such deities are associated with certain geographical areas or natural phenomena.

Ghosts are a class of spiritual beings that are often believed to cause harm. These often result from a 'bad death' including suicide, murder, execution or untimely demise. Such deaths may lead to considerable fear, for example, a house may be abandoned lest the ghost return. Many societies believe that ghosts materialise in some form that can be seen by the living. Another common belief is the possibility of a person becoming possessed by a wandering ghost. A *bhut* in India may lay hold of any passer-by. It is said to "lay hold of" the person and the victim has to resort to exorcism for deliverance.

An important question that must be considered is how these spiritual beings are conceived within Christian theology. Paul addresses this issue in 1 Corinthians 8 and 10. He affirms that there is no

God but one (8:4). He recognises the existence of other "gods" and "lords", but in a qualitatively different way. Are they manifestations of Satan and his demons in that local society? Can we say that Satan can contextualise himself in the religious beliefs of the people?

Often, when a society has converted to Christianity, Christian translators have used the name of the High God to translate the word Yahweh in the Scriptures. The lesser deities are usually ignored, being considered as some manifestation of demons. Occasionally a particular deity has been associated with Satan. This cosmological dualism has often caused considerable difficulties because the people have previously thought of spiritual beings as morally ambivalent beings.

Human Beings

A distinction is often made between witchcraft and sorcery. Although this distinction is useful as a starting point, it is necessary to recognise that in many societies no such simple separation can be made.

Among some African peoples, *witchcraft* is seen as the cause of most misfortunes including sickness, accident, crop failures, hunting failures and any general lack of success. The notion of coincidence or probability does not provide a sufficient reason for these types of failures. There must be an answer as to *why* they happen to this individual and, for some, witchcraft is the 'obvious' answer.

Most missionaries who came to sub-Saharan Africa from Europe in the nineteenth century were imbued with a critical perspective, especially about witchcraft. Witchcraft was not believed to exist, so Christians were expected to ignore it. Where Christianity became the dominant force in a society, this view was outwardly accepted, but often belief in witchcraft was merely driven underground.

A second position that has been adopted by Christian missionaries, mainly from Pentecostal churches, is that witchcraft is demonic and the accused needs to be delivered. Today, among the charismatic churches in many areas of the world, witchcraft is dealt with by vigorous prayer leading to the exorcism of the spirit. Witchcraft is perceived as one of the manifestations of the work of Satan in the community and combating it is part of the Christian's spiritual warfare. It is seen as a direct encounter between the power of God and the power of evil. Public confession of sin is often required, after which the person is encouraged to receive the cleansing blood of Christ and the enduing power of the Holy Spirit.

Sorcery is the second category. It is frequently understood as different from witchcraft in that it is a deliberate, conscious act of an individual, or group of individuals, to harm another by non-empirical means. It can express itself in various forms, including the evil eye, curses and black magic. The evil eye refers to a belief that a person may have power to harm another merely by looking at her.

Core ideas of curses and blessings appear universal among human societies. To appreciate the concept behind these oral expressions, it is necessary to realise that in the traditional worldview words are not merely viewed as vibrations in the air. Words, spoken deliberately and with intention, take upon themselves a reality of their own which can bring about the desires of the speaker. The greater the personality of the speaker, the greater will be the effectiveness of the curse or blessing. Thus, if a god utters a curse, or a devotee utters one in his name, the effect will be very powerful.

Anthropologists have long noted that witchcraft and sorcery often result from the jealousy one person may have towards another. The possibility of these spiritual powers generates intense fears even in the hearts of Christian converts, and raises the question of how people achieve protection from these sources of evil.

Protection from Evil

Often, people feel the need to draw upon additional non-empirical sources for help, so they turn to *divination*. The methods used are many, but most involve some sort of ritual or spirit possession. Generally missionaries have dismissed divination as evil, but have failed to address the question of its replacement. Christians have, therefore, often been left with secularised methods of healing, education and agriculture. However, various methods of divination and foretelling the future continue in all societies!

Various means are used to protect vulnerable members of the community. Children may, for example, be protected by some ruse that seeks to make the child less attractive, less open to envy and so divert the evil eye.

Another means of protection is the use of charms. These practices are based upon an inherent belief and fear of the evil power of magic in its various forms. Frequently, the Bible comes to take the role of a new powerful charm for the young convert. What is required is not merely a response to one aspect of magic, but a radical change in worldview that sees Jesus Christ as Lord over all — visible and invisible (Col 1:16).

Where *possession* is known within a society, there is usually some indigenous means of *exorcism* to deal with the affliction. There are often recognised exorcists who know appropriate rituals and claim to be endowed by a more powerful spirit. This form of exorcism may provide some cure, but this may only be temporary.

An alternative treatment is that the person is initiated into a *possession cult*. In possession cults, the individual comes into a working relation with the afflicting spirit. The individual remains free from the recurring affliction so long as he takes part in the periodic cult-festivals. During these festivals, the person becomes possessed by the spirit, which acts out its particular character.

In folk religion, healers, whether witchdoctors, shamans, exorcists or others, play a socially positive role. Missionaries have often considered these healers their main opponents and in some cases they have been. But, sometimes they have also been the first to recognise the power of God. Christian leaders have often taken the place and role of these healers and exorcists.

Current Issues

First, forces of evil and misfortune are an integral part of folk tradition, and the people need to see Christianity as not merely a satisfying theology, but the power of God to deal with the issues they face in their world. Teaching on spiritual conflict must be part of a holistic approach to mission and theology. There is a need for an approach that relates the social, economic and personal, and not merely sees the demonic as the sole cause of evil.

49

Second, Christians have to relate to the beliefs of their own particular cultural context. Although we accept the influence of Satan within all human societies, this does not mean that he works in the same way in all societies. Accepting the ontological truth of the reality of the demonic, there is a need to appreciate the various cultural expressions as "cultural truth."

Third, the New Testament shows that converts who have been involved in magic should destroy the paraphernalia they have used. This power encounter is an essential rite of separation from old ways and entry into the new life in Christ. However, there is a danger of this being perceived as Christian magic or stimulating an unnecessary interest in spirits. God is not merely more powerful than Satan, but has a radically different nature. The Cross of Christ is the demonstration of victory through weakness, of love over hate and of God's way over that of Satan. This has to be expressed in our ministry as well.

Fourth, Christians should be aware of the changing social context throughout the world. Frequently, those accused of being witches were people on the fringes of society, such as the elderly, isolated widows or minority groups who become scapegoats for social tensions. The Christian message should result in the restoration of social harmony through reconciliation and mutual acceptance.

Fifth, one must recognise that within our global society, literature, video, and the Internet are allowing the exchange of ideas from East and West, North and South. One result is the spread of new teachings and practices that are at times highly speculative. Christians must maintain a balance between secular scepticism and the adoption of animistic beliefs.

Sixth, Christians from a background of folk religion need to develop a worldview and theology that acknowledges the demonic without letting the demonic continue to captivate them. They, like all Christians, need to have their eyes fixed upon the Lord Jesus Christ who has all power and authority. We all must be aware of the radical nature of the kingdom of God that manifests not merely the power of God, but the peace, *shalom,* of God that transforms people and societies.

6. Spiritual Conflict in the Ministry of the Church

Margaret Jacobs' paper was oriented towards outsiders in evangelism. She dealt with these questions: What is the role of spiritual conflict in the evangelistic ministry of the church, especially towards people in occult bondage, chemical dependency and the possessed? How do we prepare such ministry? What is the use of spiritual gifts in such a ministry?

It seems as though the church has a greater opportunity to minister than ever before. A critical focus is this: Who are we in Christ? This is the foundation for our ministry in spiritual conflict.

Images of ministry were drawn from Ephesians 2:19-22 and 3:10-11. Christ is the cornerstone of the church and our ministry. It is in him that the church is built and in him that we are built together to become a dwelling place in which God lives. Further, God's intent was that it is through the church (those who belong to Christ) that the rulers and authorities (human and spiritual powers) would know the manifold wisdom of God.

Mrs Jacobs noted that while the church has enjoyed the privilege of being a part of God's family and household, the church has neglected her responsibility to make known the manifold wisdom of God to the rulers and authorities in the heavenly realms, according to the eternal purpose that is accomplished in Christ Jesus. To do this, we need to start pulling down strongholds by declaring God's sovereignty over the physical, inhabited world; over the world systems and over our perception of the fleeting nature of time.

As we minister to those who face addictions, those trapped in cults and those oppressed by the demonic, in addition to knowing the biblical teaching on spiritual conflict, we also need to understand the present reality of occult activity worldwide, the enormity of the bondage to drugs and the subtlety of cult movements if we are to minister effectively.

To those who minister to the demonised, Mrs Jacobs stresses reliance on Jesus. She personally advocated the following as essentials in preparation for dealing in this ministry:

1. Completely accept Jesus' leadership in every area of our life.

2. Be willing for a total dealing of the Cross daily in our life.

3. Be willing to lay down our own lives and the lives of our loved ones (Matt 10:37-38).

4. Learn to hear the Lord speak to us in our spirit (John 16:12-14).

5. Learn how to bring our mind captive to Christ's leading (2 Cor 10:3-5; Rom 12:2).

6. Memorise key scriptures and understand them (2 Tim 3:16; 2 Tim 2:15).

7. Be subject to God's delegated authority.

8. Never underestimate Satan's power (1 Peter 5:8).

Worship and Prayer

Juliet Thomas presented an Indian perspective on the realities of worship and prayer as key components in spiritual conflict. She noted that in the process of sanctification, we face three enemies, not just one: the world, the flesh and the Devil. We are not to be conformed to the ways of the world, we are to crucify the flesh and we must resist the Devil. The whole conflict we are facing is a conflict between two kingdoms, and Christians have been transferred from one kingdom (of darkness) to another (the kingdom of the Son God loves).

Worship is critical to us because our lives take place in the world — which lowers our spiritual energy. Worship brings us back to perspective through having spent time in his presence — which restores in a way nothing else can. Worship is not something just seen in certain times (whether morning or evening), but a continuous act expressed in the idea of abiding in Jesus Christ. Our abiding is to be continuous rather than periodic; and our worship is to likewise be an abiding one, permeating the whole of our lives.

2 Timothy 3:1-5 indicates four types of lovers: lovers of self, lovers of money, lovers of pleasure and lovers of God. Mrs Thomas noted that lovers of spiritual warfare also face the danger of losing track of pursuing loving God and being holy. Today, many evangelicals tend to be motivated by the results in terms of numbers, rather than holy lives before God — worship is the missing jewel in modern evangelicalism.

What is worship? It defies adequate definition. Worship is all that we are, responding to all that God is. It is learning to be still — not focused in activity and motion. We do not worship God so that our requests will be granted, but for who the Lord is and who we were made to be. Worship is not only individual — it is corporate.

The nature of worship is seen through the many examples in the Bible. Mrs Thomas focused on the passage of Jesus and the Samaritan woman as an example of teaching about worship (John 4). Jesus indicates that God wants a special type of worship: it must be in spirit and in truth, a challenge in our post-modern culture (which denies absolute truth). In his teaching, Christ changed worship. Now, place and locality mean nothing. To worship God in spirit means to worship with the spiritual whole of one's being and personality, trusting the Lord in all areas of life. Worshiping in truth means that we worship with our minds; we approach God in the true way through Jesus, as expressed in the Word. Symbols of place and time are no longer needed; we are to do away with them as a necessity for worship.

Further, Jesus teaches that God is seeking true worshipers. The Holy Spirit has been sent by Christ to indwell and empower us to be true worshipers. Romans 12:1 commands us to offer our bodies as living sacrifices, indicating that worship is costly. Our bodies need to be pure before God, including what we do with our hands, eyes and mouths. Romans 12:2 commands us to be transformed by the renewing of our minds; the mind is where the battle is today. In Philippians, Paul tells us how to worship with our minds: by keeping our minds focused on Christ (Phil 2) and centring our minds on what is true, noble, right, pure, lovely and admirable (4:8).

Corporate prayer is also important. 2 Chronicles 7:14 explains why our countries are in such desperate trouble — the church is not humbling itself before God and turning from the ways of wickedness.

We are in spiritual warfare, but there are many ways to address that warfare. It need not be violent, it need not be spectacular, but it should be based on God's leading and the ways the Spirit enables us.

Sometimes God wants to keep us unhealed so that we lean on the Lord, as seen in Joni Ericson-Tada's life. Joni has learned to draw closer to God *because* of her handicap.

Sometimes God allows us to die for him, as in the Australian missionary and sons who were burned to death in India. At the funeral, the wife's first words were "I forgive those who killed my husband and sons." That one simple message of Christ's love touched India more deeply than any signs and wonders ever have, a truth we should not overlook.

7. The Issue of Territorial Spirits

One of the major theological and strategic issues in the evangelical missionary movement worldwide in recent years is the discussion of the role of so-called "territorial spirits" in spiritual warfare. Dr A. Scott Moreau and Dr Charles Kraft dealt with this issue from somewhat different perspectives. The following section is primarily based on their papers.

Background

Pentecostals and charismatics have, from the start of their movements, dealt with *demonisation* or *possession*. They believe (together with many other evangelical and Catholic Christians) that demons may enter a person and cause great harm that will only go away when the demons are expelled. Demons are seen as independent, spiritual entities under the authority of Satan, active both in tempting and pushing people to do evil and in extreme cases possessing people. Spiritual conflict for these groups, then, includes both dealing with temptations and expelling demons. They also regularly engage in praying for physical healing and in intercessory prayer. The charismatic movement also included *inner healing* among the activities. Then some representatives of what is often called the Third Wave of spiritual renewal, starting in the 1980s, added *cosmic-level spiritual warfare* against *territorial spirits* to the list of forms of spiritual warfare.

C. Peter Wagner, a leading representative for the Third Wave, says that in engaging territorial spirits as part of the ministry of setting people free to respond to the gospel, we have introduced a "spiritual technology" which will bring the greatest power boost in the mission of the church since William Carey started the Protestant mission movement at the end of the eighteenth century.

In a nutshell, what Mr Wagner and others are calling "strategic-level spiritual warfare" (SLSW), is praying against these territorial spirits, seeking to "map" their strategies over given locations by discerning their names and what they use to keep people in bondage and then to bind them in turn so that evangelism may go unhindered. The idea of "spiritual mapping" is one in which people research an area and try to identify the spirit(s) who are in charge over it. Prayer then may loosen the hold of territorial spirits so the people in the given area may then come to Christ more freely.

A Theological Foundation?

In an attempt to build a theological foundation for these views and practices, it is argued that Satan is not omnipotent or omniscient, which are attributes of God alone. Thus, Satan can only wield his power by delegating it to spirit helpers who work out his schemes in local contexts. They must be organised in some fashion, or else chaos would dominate Satan's efforts to rule the world. Jesus had to bind the strong man before he could plunder the strong man's house (Matt 12:29). Mr Wagner interprets: "The 'house' is the territory controlled by Satan, or his delegated spirits, and that territory cannot be taken unless he is bound. But once the territorial spirits are bound, the kingdom of God can flow into the territory and 'plunder the strong man's goods,' as it were."

There are several biblical passages that appear to relate demons to territories. In the Old Testament, there is the concept of gods of the nations exercising power in specific geographic localities, eg, the 'gods' of the hills versus 'gods' of the plains (1 Kings 20:23). The most commonly cited example is Daniel 10:1-11:1, in which the princes of Persia and Greece appear to be demons in charge of the respective geopolitical units. Finally, another example is the demons begging Jesus not to send them out of an area (Mark 5:10).

These views have, however, not been left unchallenged. The existence of territorial spirits, as defined by the spiritual warfare movement, has been strongly opposed. Perhaps the most thorough critique is provided by Chuck Lowe, who concludes: "The evidence cited for SLSW is unconvincing. Scripture provides no support, animism is an unreliable guide and the 'case study' evidence is anecdotal rather than verified."

The Core Ideas and Strategies

A whole new vocabulary has been coined to distinguish strategies, characters, practices and issues related to territorial spirits. Before evaluating such practices associated with territorial spirits, we need to explain them.

Levels of Spiritual Warfare

C. Peter Wagner has developed an approach to spiritual warfare that involves three levels. The first is *ground-level spiritual warfare*, which refers to casting demons out of believers. The second is *occult-level spiritual warfare*, which refers to "dealing with powers of darkness that are more co-ordinated and organised than one or more demons who might happen to be afflicting a certain person at a certain time." The third is *strategic-level spiritual warfare*, which "...involves confrontation with the high-ranking territorial spirits which have been assigned by Satan to coordinate the activities of the kingdom of darkness over a certain area in order to keep the people's minds blinded to the 'gospel of the glory of Christ' as we read in 2 Corinthians 4:3-4."

Dr Kraft, in contrast to Mr Wagner, presents two levels: *ground-level warfare* and *cosmic-level warfare*. He classifies spirits in different categories, and in each category assumes that there are spirits assigned by Satan and competing spirits (angels) assigned by God. On God's side there are angels and archangels (Dan 10:13, 21). On Satan's side there are "spiritual forces of evil in the heavenly places": rulers, authorities, cosmic powers of this present darkness (Eph 6:12). He further assumes that cosmic-level spirits have a good bit of authority over ground-level spirits, probably assigning them and ruling over them, and that cosmic-level spirits gain and maintain their rights only through human permission.

Prayer Journeys

Prayer journeys are essentially field trips to practise prayer walking and, in some cases, to enable better spiritual mapping. Taken as short-term mission trips, they include short visits to strategic cities or sections of cities within a country or continent. Prayer journeys focus on praying on-site and do not entail evangelism or mercy ministries.

Spiritual Mapping

One result of this emphasis on territorial spirits is the development of a strategy for evangelism known as spiritual mapping. George Otis, who coined the phrase, notes:

> "Spiritual mapping is a means by which we can see what is beneath the surface of the material world; but it is not magic. It is subjective in that it is a skill born out of a right relationship with God and a love for His world. It is objective in that it can be verified (or discredited) by history, sociological observation and God's Word."

Harold Caballeros concisely summarises the underlying thinking:

> "Spiritual mapping helps us identify the strong man. In some cases, spiritual mapping will give us a series of characteristics that will guide us directly to the territorial prince or power. In other cases, we will find ourselves facing a natural person whom Satan is using. In still others, we will find ourselves face-to-face with a corrupt social structure."

Wagner advocates on a city-wide level to "work with intercessors especially gifted and called to strategic-level spiritual warfare, seeking God's revelation of: (a) the redemptive gift(s) of the city; (b) Satan's strongholds; (c) territorial spirits assigned to the city; (d) corporate sin; and (e) God's plan of attack and timing."

Finally, some emphasise a need to discover the names of the territorial spirits as part of the spiritual mapping process, whether through historical or religious research or by revelation through prayer.

Approaches to Confronting Territorial Spirits

For those who assert that the concept of territorial spirits is biblical, and that we have a responsibility to work against their efforts, a spectrum of prayer approaches may be used.

Confronters

The more aggressive advocates promote direct and public confrontation of the identified territorial spirits to weaken their hold on the location and enable greater evangelisation. In addition to personal prayer against such spirits by specially anointed individuals, they organise spiritual mapping projects, prayer journeys and sometimes local praise marches or rallies as means of confrontation.

Moderates

The more moderate emphasise unity of local leadership, centrality of prayer and priority of dealing with strongholds within the church as preconditions for aggressive prayer against the strongholds.

Conservatives

Though acknowledging that there is scriptural evidence of territorial spirits, the conservative maintain that we do not see in Scripture or church history specific SLSW encounters of the type being described today. They advocate an approach closer to the truth encounter in which the local body of Christ manifests repentance and reconciliation in a way that speaks destruction to the powers of darkness. This approach is modelled on Paul's letter to the Ephesians.

Response: Points of Appreciation

Dr Moreau had several points of appreciation for those who advocate SLSW. First, SLSW and the emphasis on territorial spirits take Satan and the powers more seriously than traditional Western approaches. It advocates focus on the power of prayer, rather than merely on planning and strategy. This is a healthy corrective for much Western management-oriented missiology.

Because of the focus on the spiritual, advocates of SLSW recognise that divisiveness weakens prayer and, as a result, they stress the unity of the church in fulfilling its mission. They seek co-operation, rather than competition.

There can be no doubt that SLSW advocates focus on the ultimate goal of saving the lost. Many of the proponents emphasise that the ultimate goal is not casting down spirits, but bringing the lost to Christ.

Another helpful feature is recognition of the evil spiritual dimensions of a culture. All cultures have elements that together work as domination systems that entrap people and keep them blinded to spiritual realities.

One of the emphases of those engaged in this type of ministry is to discern areas in which the church needs to repent. Often, this comes together with the call for a public gathering to express corporate repentance. Certainly, this is a positive action which unleashes the power of God to work powerfully in a location or people.

There is generally an explicit recognition that this concept or strategy is new and pioneering, rather than proven. Advocates see themselves, in some respects, as experimenters who are following God's leading.

Response: Points of Disagreement

Dr Moreau also pointed out several areas where he disagrees with SLSW. First, whatever our conclusion as to whether or not spirits are assigned territories is, perhaps the biggest obstacle to SLSW is that the fundamental strategy *is not found in the Bible* or in church history, at least not without some serious stretching of the accounts.

The emphasis on discerning and naming demons before we can have power over them is approaching a form of Christian animism or Christian magic. The idea of needing the names to have power over spirits is found in magical thinking around the world. The concept of "discerning" the names and the functions will always be subjective at best.

Prayer was not intended to be a sophisticated spiritual "weapon," but a means of fellowship, growth and strength. One danger of an attitude of "spiritual violence" is that we may become the very thing we are fighting against. Tom White, one of the more cautious advocates, comments:

> "The primary activity envisioned in strategic warfare is intercession before the throne of God, not interaction with

fallen principalities. We are not called to wield laser beams of biblical authority to destroy heavenly strongholds. We are called to destroy in people's lives (Christian and non-Christian) 'strongholds ... arguments and every proud obstacle raised up against the knowledge of God' (2 Cor 10:4-5)."

As important as informed prayer is, seeking information about the spirit realm as a means of overcoming the evil powers or gaining special knowledge does not appear to be portrayed as necessary (or even significant) in Scripture. Indeed, the majority of the warnings against the occult in the Bible focus on unwarranted explorations into the spiritual realms for knowledge or power.

Ultimately, a focus on this strategy as the key to effective evangelisation demeans the Scriptures: if this strategy is *so* significant, then why is it not found in the Bible? Additionally, support for this strategy has tended to come through reading into biblical texts the meanings that advocates of SLSW want. For example, the struggle against "rulers" and "authorities" in Paul's statement in Ephesians 6:12 is not an advocacy of warfare directly against territorial spirits. The statement comes in the context of the Christian's daily struggle, not the church's SLSW strategy.

Another possible danger is that we detach demons from people, which de-emphasises our own participation in the rebellion against God. In concentrating on finding out the various forms of territorial demonic attachments and focusing our attention on them, we ignore the fact that all too often the enemy is *us*. If the enemy is both within us, as sin we need to repent of, and outside us, as demonic agencies, methodologies that ignore the inside are doomed to failure in the long run. We must consider the possibility that the greater bondage may rest with the wickedness of human hearts.

Finally, the idea of serving notice, evicting and binding spirits over territories does not have biblical warrant and carries too much emphasis on technique and effectiveness. How can we serve notice to a spirit over a territory, if the people themselves continue to invite control by the way they live?

Response: Some Suggestions

The first suggestion in this area is that we must be more *cautious* and not use exaggerated claims and anecdotes as the means by which SLSW is established. We must be careful in analysing the success stories given in the literature and not confuse coincidence with causation. While there may be reports of crime rates declining over a period coinciding with a particular prayer struggle, this does not prove that it was the struggle itself that resulted in the decline. It is also important not to base conclusions on mere hearsay, but on thoroughly verified sources.

A second suggestion is to emphasise spiritual *diagnosis* over spiritual mapping and be more cautious in our pronouncements. We must enable Christians to develop a worldview that acknowledges the powers without being captivated by an unhealthy interest in them. We should keep our attention on God's sovereign control and use this sovereignty as a lens through which we examine demonic activities. Surely, this is a significant theme in Ephesians, as Paul notes Christ's authority over every name that can be named in any age (1:21) and prays that the Ephesians would be filled with God's power — not to confront demons — but to know the depths of God's love (3:14-19). Along these lines, we should find appropriate ways to stress more strongly the need for discipleship, not just warfare.

Additionally, we must not overlook the need to die to the powers, rather than follow the desire to overcome them. We need to die not only to our privatised egos, but to the outer network of social beliefs also. In self-denial, the task is not a conquest of ego by ego, but one of ego-surrender to God's redemptive initiative.

Finally, our goal must be to integrate the spiritual, the personal, the cultural and the social and to stop placing all blame on the spirits and start recognising the human side of choice to rebel against God's will.

8. Spiritual Conflict in Socio-political Contexts

A major concern of the consultation was to relate the theme "Deliver Us From Evil" to the total human reality, both the personal and social dimensions. A paper by Dr Knud Jørgensen was devoted to the conflict with evil, as it manifests itself in the socio-political realm. He defined his task in the following terms:

> "My brief is to focus on evil and Satan, as they are manifested in the socio-political realm, both collectively and individually, in such evils as injustice, exploitation, oppression, materialism, war, ethnic hatred, persecution, destruction of humans and of creation. How can the Evil One be identified and fought in this realm?"

Need for a Broad Perspective on Spiritual Conflict

Evangelical theology usually views the conflict between Jesus and his adversary as a conflict between two kingdoms, a hostile realm in conflict with the kingdom of God. This hostile realm has several dimensions or fronts, including, what Dr Moreau calls, the systemic front, where the agenda is warfare against the domination systems that make up our cultures and societies. These systems (cultural, economic, political, religious) are manifestations of what the New Testament calls "the world" (Greek: *kosmos*): "The whole world lies under the power of the evil one" (1 John 5:19; cf John 12:31 and 14:30 where Jesus calls Satan "the ruler of this world"). This concept of kingdoms in conflict is also illustrated by Satan's claim of dominion when he offered Jesus the kingdoms of the world (Matt 4:8-9). The point is clearly that even though God ultimately is the sovereign king of heaven and earth, Satan does exercise significant influence over *kosmos* and its power structures.

The conflict is evidenced in the tension between the two, often overlapping, kingdoms. Our allegiance is to the kingdom of God and, as citizens of this kingdom, we are part of the new creation.

Nevertheless, we see the impact of evil all around us, in the form of violence, poverty, crime, racism, ethnic strife, betrayal and brokenness.

It is essential that we perceive evil and spiritual conflict in a broad way. It has to do with our common struggle as Christians and touches every area of our lives — family, relations, neighbours, communities and work. All of these areas of life are battlegrounds for the kingdoms in conflict.

We also need to bring along a balanced view of evil influences: the biblical perspective highlights the interconnectedness of the flesh, the world and the Devil. In this context, we use the term *world* to signify the ungodly aspects of culture — values and traditions that stand contrary to biblical understanding. Satan attempts to exert influence on the societal and cultural levels. This influence may come through direct idolatry and occult practices and beliefs, or it may come through what Sherwood Lingenfelter calls "prisons of disobedience" that are found in all societies. In a sense, every culture and system may be used by the Evil One to hold us in bondage by entangling us in a life of conformity to shared values and beliefs that are fundamentally contrary to God's purpose and will for humanity.

This link between culture/society and bondage emphasises that how the bondage is experienced will vary from culture to culture. The main bondage most Westerners — or should we say "the westernised/ globalised world" — experience is still the desire for affluence. The globalised culture has allowed the "pursuit of the good life" to shape the perspective, values and psychology so profoundly that Lesslie Newbigin may be right in viewing the Western culture as the most non-Christian culture ever.

Engaging the Powers

In the conflict between the kingdoms, we are, as Paul says (Eph 6:10-20), confronted by rulers (*archai*), authorities (*exousiai*), cosmic powers (*kosmokratores*) and spiritual forces (*pneumatika*). Among evangelicals, these terms are usually understood to refer to Satanic forces. Paul's focus is here in the day-to-day struggle of the believer in the midst of culture and society. We will just call them the Powers. In the following sections, there will be a particular focus on the works of Walter Wink, a theologian who looks at these Powers in a different way — namely as created, fallen, but redeemable.

In addition to a trilogy on the Powers, Mr Wink has published a condensed and popularised version under the title *The Powers That Be* (1998). Mr Wink's aim, particularly in the condensed version, is to help us reformulate ancient concepts, such as God and Satan, angels and demons, principalities and powers, in light of the world today. The refreshing and provocative aspect of Mr Wink's work is his contextualisation of powers and principalities in the midst of our contemporary social institutions. Mr Wink is as concerned with salvation as with justice.

His point of departure is that everything has both a physical and a spiritual aspect. Therefore, the Powers are not simply people and their institutions; they also include the spirituality at the core of those institutions. If we want to change those systems — social, economic, cultural, political — we must address not only the outer form, but the inner spirit as well. Mr Wink claims that every business, corporation, school and bureaucracy is a combination of visible and invisible, outer and inner, physical and spiritual. However, this spirituality is not always benign. The sole purpose of the institutions is to serve the general welfare; when they refuse to do so, their spirituality becomes diseased (demonic). The demons are not up there, but over here, in the socio-spiritual structures and political systems. When these powers (which may be personal or impersonal) network around idolatrous values, we get what Mr Wink calls "the Domination System" whose master is Satan. In this way, the Powers are everywhere around us, and their presence is inescapable. Our task is to unmask this idolatry and recall the Powers to their created purposes in the world. This, however, requires the ministry of the church (Eph 3:10) and not just individuals. It is, therefore, the task of the church to remind eg, economic corporations that as creatures of God they have, as their divine vocation, the achievement of human well-being.

So the evil is not intrinsic, but rather the result of idolatry. This in turn means that the task of redemption is not restricted to changing individuals, but also to changing the fallen institutions. Mr Wink takes one more step: the gospel is not the message about the salvation of individuals from the world, but news about a world transfigured, right down to its basic structures. This cosmic salvation will take place when God gathers up all things in Christ (Eph 1:10).

It is not difficult to question some of Mr Wink's assumptions and views. How does he understand the Fall? He may describe evil with terrible "human" examples, but one wonders whether evil really stands in contrast and absolute opposition to the living God. "Fallenness does not touch our essence, but it characterises our existence." In the same way, one is left uncertain as to whether, after the Fall, the human being was totally alienated from God. True, Mr Wink talks clearly about the need for the individual to be changed; human misery is caused by institutions, but these institutions are maintained by human beings, ie, the institutions are made evil by us. Yet, we lack a more clear understanding and description of the gulf between God and humans caused by disobedience and sin.

Nevertheless, Mr Wink's thinking challenges us to bring together evangelism and social struggle and to include in our evangelistic task the proclamation to the Powers of the manifold wisdom of God.

Fighting the Powers

The fight against the Powers has already been under way a long time by our engaging them and diagnosing their strategies and delusions.

We may disagree on several accounts with Mr Wink's interpretation of God's reign — but there is, for us evangelicals, a serious challenge in his attempt *to place God's reign in a socio-political and cultural setting*. Without such daring contextualisations, we run the risk of transforming the gospel into a timeless, placeless, eternal nowhere. The challenge for us, as we fight the Powers, is to proclaim the gospel as a context-specific remedy for the evils of a society and a culture dominated by the Powers.

The primary weapon against the Powers has always been and will always remain the liberating message of Jesus. The gospel is the most powerful antidote for domination that the world has ever known. It was that antidote that inspired the abolition of slavery; the women's movement; the non-violence movement; the civil rights movement; the human rights movement; the fall of Nazism, Fascism and Communism; and the break-up of apartheid.

In our fight against the Powers, we shall lift up the biblical focus of *servanthood* and *servant leadership* (Luke 22:22-27), not just as a principle, but because the central core of the gospel is the Servant of the Lord who took upon himself our transgressions.

The Cross in Spiritual Conflict

Paul claims that it was not primarily through the resurrection that the Powers were unmasked, but on and through the Cross: "He set this aside, nailing it to the Cross. He disarmed the rulers and authorities and make a public example of them, triumphing over them in it" (Col 2:14-15). Jesus died because he challenged the Powers. But something went wrong for the Powers. Nailing him to the cross meant the end of their own power. Therefore on the Cross, the Powers themselves are paraded and made captive. The power of God is here, hidden under seeming powerlessness (*sub contrarie specie*).

And so, the Cross continues to challenge, because the Cross reveals the delusions and deceptions. It reveals that death does not have the final word and that truth cannot be killed. It is now possible to enter any darkness and trust God to wrestle from it resurrection.

So let us continue to lift up the Cross of Christ because we know that where the Cross is lifted high, the Powers are losing strength. This is meant in a very literal sense: Proclaim the Cross to the leaders of this world, shout it out in the midst of our modern consumer temples, walk into the battle zones with the Cross of reconciliation, challenge fighting in the name of Christus Victor. In doing so, let us die with Christ. We need to understand better what Jesus meant by losing one's life: "Those who try to make their life secure will lose it, but those who lose their life will keep it" (Luke 17:33).

The primary task of the church, with reference to the Powers, is to unmask their idolatrous pretensions, to identify their dehumanising values, to strip from them the mantle of credibility and to set free their victims. This includes the testimony of the crucified Christ. It does not include a commission to create a new society.

Our offer of praise and worship to the one true God stands central in calling the Powers' bluff because in and through that praising of the one true God, the bluff of all idols is revealed. So, as we fight the Powers, we shall ascribe to God glory and strength.

9. Spiritual Conflict in Light of Psychology and Medicine

A major issue in the debate over spiritual conflict is the relation between the spiritual and the psychological. This becomes especially acute when Christians, on the basis of the Bible or contemporary experience, claim that the Devil and demons are ontologically real spiritual beings that may influence people, even possess them, and may be resisted or even exorcised by the use of merely spiritual means.

The question may be raised whether phenomena, such as possession, belong in a purely religious and spiritual realm and should be dealt with accordingly, or are symptoms of psychological or somatic disturbances that should be dealt with by the medical and psychological professions. Sometimes, one must be able to distinguish between spiritual and medical or psychological afflictions; at other times a combination of the two approaches may be needed to alleviate the suffering.

The consultation deemed it essential that this issue be addressed not only by theologians or religious practitioners, but also by a competent Christian psychologist. Such a person is Dr Jerry Mungadze who gave the paper on this topic.

Spiritual Conflict and Psychological, Psychiatric and Physiological Illness

Sometimes, those who are convinced of the reality of spiritual conflict tend to minimise the reality of psychological and psychiatric illness. The result is that often Christians and others suffering from psychological illness have been treated as if they were demonised. The reality of evil spiritual forces is undisputed both in the Old and New Testaments. In the New Testament, there are several examples of demonic forces causing physical and mental affliction. The real question is not whether spiritual conflict exists, but what is the best way of dealing with it when it may co-exist with psychological, psychiatric and physical illness. This is further complicated by the fact that there are times when psychological illness exists with no direct link to the spiritual realm. In such cases, assuming the presence of spiritual causes may lead to serious mistakes in helping others.

Genesis 3 outlines the Fall of the human race and the entrance of sin, death, pain, suffering and illness into the world. The fallen world we live in is subject to natural laws. Psychology and medicine help us deal with our problems related to the natural laws. Our minds or souls contain our decision-making capacity, our desires, our will and our emotions. This is where psychological processes take place.

Medicine helps us with problems related to the body. The body has many organs, including the brain, which is the powerhouse of most bodily functions. The brain regulates certain chemical processes in the body for our survival and sustenance.

It is very unfortunate that the Western worldview seems to split the person into separate parts, such as body and mind or material and immaterial. It appears, from a biblical viewpoint, that body, soul and spirit are so intertwined that they cannot be separated. This unity also makes it difficult to tell when certain problems are largely psychological, psychiatric, physical or spiritual. This brings us to the discussion on correct discernment and diagnosis.

Discernment and Correct Diagnosis

One of the fundamentals in dealing with people is that no harm should be done to people in the name of deliverance or help. If someone is having problems with physical manifestations, it could be a physical condition that needs a physician's attention. Ignoring this could lead to death or physical impairment for the person seeking help. Physical manifestations *need to be followed up with questions concerning the presence of a history of physical disease* in the person or the family, and also by a *visit to a physician*. The next area, which possibly presents the hardest challenge, is the manifestation of what could be mental illness or a demonic affliction. The safest approach is to *first rule out mental illness or psychological problems* before assuming that it is a spiritual problem. The following should be taken into account:

1. We need to ask for a history of mental problems.

2. We need to check for distress of an emotional or mental nature in the person's life.

3. We need to find out if the person has previously sought psychological or psychiatric help or help from traditional healers.

4. We also need to know if the person is using psychiatric medications or if he or she has ever received them before.

5. We need to see if they have been hospitalised for emotional or mental problems in the past.

If the information given seems to contain these natural situations listed above, then the person needs psychological or psychiatric care even if they have already been through deliverance or prayer.

Special Attention: Dissociative Identity Disorder

There is one *mental illness* that is perhaps the most often misunderstood as demonisation by those engaged in Christian deliverance. This illness is called Dissociative Identity Disorder, and was formerly known as Multiple Personality Disorder. The afflicted person may hears voices; see people and things no one else sees; speak in different voices; have memory lapses too great to be accounted for by ordinary forgetfulness; engage in self-destructive behaviour; and have unexplainable physical symptoms.

Sometimes people with this illness are convinced that they are demon-possessed. The voices they hear claim to be demons when they actually are not. In North America, this mental illness is generally well understood and has been successfully treated. In the majority of third world countries, it is largely seen as spirit possession or ancestral mediumistic activities. Usually in these societies, people with this condition go through traditional healing or Christian exorcism. This actually antagonises the created personas and makes them more angry and destructive towards the person who is afflicted. The following are helpful guidelines when dealing with people who claim to be demonised.

1. If the person who claims to be demonised is also a victim of childhood trauma, the person may have this disorder.

2. Although these so-called "created parts" claim to be separate people, they are not foreign beings, but really parts of the person's mind created unknowingly to deal with the trauma. Therefore these parts need to be embraced rather than cast out. The person must be encouraged to realise there is only one real person.

3. This type of disorder needs to be treated by specially trained professionals. When ministering to a person with dissociative disorders, it is best to work together with such a trained professional.

4. Occasionally, these created personas do not share the same beliefs, behaviours, or perceptions with the main person. As a result, usually some type of conflict arises. If the person is a Christian, it is important to know it does not mean that he or she is lost, but just very unstable.

Every so often this illness will exist together with a spiritual conflict. In such cases, deliverance is not effective if the existence of the illness is ignored.

Case Study: Seminary Student

A seminary student believed that he was possessed by a legion of demons that yelled obscenities to him daily and told him to get out of seminary. Sometimes, he heard little boys crying and adult voices screaming. He had been through many deliverance sessions. According to some of his ministers, he had been delivered from the spirits of anger, hate, suicide and lust. But, he still heard voices. He would again experience the same problems. After encouragement from his wife, the man sought therapy from the seminary counselling centre and was referred to a trauma specialist. Here, it was discovered that the voices belonged to created parts inside called "alter personalities," not demons. The personalities carried different emotions that developed because of early childhood abuse. Some acted out in anger and some in hatred. Some even wanted to die because they were so wounded by the abuse.

Caution Required

Given the controversial nature of our particular topic, a few appropriate cautions should be taken. At times, various deliverance approaches go overboard when diagnosing people with demonic problems when they actually have emotional and psychological problems. Some even go so far as to believe that any emotional problem invites demonic forces. We have heard of demons of anger, lust, eating, suicide, depression, anxiety, and so on. Some of these "demons" are actually psychological illnesses. Others make it sound as if it does not take much for demonic forces to invade people's lives. It is helpful to realise that demonic strongholds are often connected to covenants and pacts with evil forces rather than fleeting brushes with evil. The excessive emphasis on demonising seems to cheapen the validity of the safety that is found in the blood and name of the Lord Jesus Christ. It can also lead to an over-spiritualisation of emotional and psychiatric problems.

When considering the possibility of demonisation, it is therefore important to obtain the following information from the persons seeking help:

1. Do they have any involvement in the occult or cultic practices?

2. Did anyone in their family line practice occultism or cultic arts?

3. Have they willingly, under any circumstances, vowed to follow Satan?

4. Did anyone dedicate them to Satan or some other god, spirit or any being when they were children?

These types of experiences indicate that the person may indeed be involved in a spiritual conflict, which would need attention immediately. If it becomes obvious that a person is in a spiritual crisis, it should be remembered that people need to be empowered to fight their own battles instead of relying on an outsider to do it for them.

People need to take responsibility for their situations. They should renounce whatever pacts or covenants were made. They need to fully recognise what happened, how it happened and repent of it. As believers they have the authority to remove their loyalty from Satan and to trust God.

Collaboration Between Mental Health and Spiritual Ministry

The seeming conflict between theology and psychology is nothing new. Recently, however, there seems to be a growing understanding that the two can be in collaboration. As the church seeks to evangelise the world, it faces challenges in the people it seeks to reach. Woundedness is a common reality in the world today. Abuse, poverty, war, disease and serious occult practices cause all kinds of spiritual and emotional problems for people. Mental health sciences have done helpful research in this area that can help the church better understand wounded people and how they react to certain situations. Research has shown that when people are traumatised during childhood, certain biological alterations occur in the way their brain processes information. These alterations can severely impact the way these people function in society, which includes the church. Some of the following problems are examples of what wounded people may experience:

1. Inability to control emotions and negative behaviours,

2. Inability to rationalise,

3. Severe panic attacks, and

4. Memory problems.

Research has discovered that the structures in the left hemisphere of the brain process our rational thinking, organisation and analysing. These may be significantly reduced in activity, thus making trauma victims unable to be rational when they are reminded of past trauma. When victims are in those situations, they are extremely emotional, making it hard to reason with them.

If the people who are going through deliverance prayer happen to be victims of trauma, chances are they may respond to any threatening or disturbing stimuli as if the trauma is happening all over again. In such a case, the person becomes re-traumatised by the deliverance instead of receiving help.

This is a typical scenario when dealing with wounded people who may seem to be angry, aggressive and demon-possessed. Given this situation, it would appear that to approach wounded people effectively, especially in the light of world evangelism, we would need collaboration between mental health and spiritual ministry. These two disciplines look at people and the world as different from each other. Each can contribute to what the other does not know much about.

There are certain things we need to know about *people* in order to help them:

1. People are complex. They cannot be easily explained in one dimension, such as spiritual or psychological. People are impacted by their heredity, culture, environment, geography and new birth.

2. People are not always aware of the processes at work in them. Therefore, denial of certain realities could be due to unawareness, instead of pure denial or resistance.

3. People are more than what we can see and touch; there is an element of spiritual essence that science cannot put a finger on. Reducing our understanding of people and the world to only what can be seen, only diminishes our ability to reach people who are open to the reality of the unseen.

A comprehensive understanding of people and the world they live in can only enhance whatever type of ministry or secular work one does. The church should be no exception. It needs to develop an awareness of different people and their different worlds.

Concluding Proposals

World evangelisation is more complex today because we are aware that humans have become more complex. Sometimes, the church has sought to use worldly means to reach humans in their complexity, but without the power of God this is futile. At other times, the church ignores the complexity of human beings, over-spiritualises and is, therefore, not producing lasting results. We propose a strong collaboration between Christian mental health workers, pastors and evangelists to help meet the needs of the whole person in a holistic way. Practically, this collaboration may be done in several different ways: Christian mental health workers and church ministers may hold joint seminars on issues related to spiritual growth and the mental health field. Churches may also engage mental health staff to minister to the wounded people.

Some of these ideas are already being put into practice in some countries. They need, however, to be spread in those countries that do not yet know or practise them.

10. Contextualisation of Spiritual Conflict

Dr Marguerite Kraft's paper focused on issues of contextualisation and spiritual conflict. She noted that there are many societies that are spirit-power oriented and daily life in many of these societies involves finding a way to balance the powers so as not to disrupt life.

The field of anthropology has provided many definitions for worldview, the central control box of culture. Worldview, as Dr Kraft used it, refers to the basic assumptions, values and allegiances of a group of people. In many societies of the world, supernaturalism is the centre of life and the integrating factor. Humans are seen as weak and needing increased strength to survive in a world full of spirit activity. In such societies, spiritual power is viewed as necessary for success, wealth, guidance and meeting daily crises, eg, illness, accidents, barrenness, drought. In her research, she heard several questions coming from the minds and hearts of Christians or potential Christians from other societies: Does the foreign doctor know how to take care of the spirits who are making me ill? How will I know when to plant my crops if I do not go to the local diviner? Does the pastor have enough spiritual power to deal with my wife's barrenness? How can I survive the curses of my father when he hears of my Christian faith? Where, within the church, is there power to protect me from witches? In fact, when discussing Christianity with a non-believer from another society, the question raised is often not, "Who is this Jesus?" but "What can Jesus do?" In reflecting, Dr Kraft considered the validity and significance of this question.

Human beings seem to know they have limitations and seek help beyond their own capabilities. Each society has its own way of obtaining spiritual power for times and events that are filled with unknown dangers and for situations that are beyond human control. In many societies of the world, the quest for spiritual power in daily living is at the forefront of people's minds. Dr Kraft used the term "spiritual-power oriented" to describe such societies.

In her research of concepts of spiritual power in three different societies, she found that spiritual power was sought for basic human needs. *Perpetuity needs* included ensuring fertility for reproduction within the family and also as it relates to the land, crops and livestock. *Prosperity needs* included the dangerous transitions through life (eg, childbirth, puberty, marriage, death) as well as building a new house, opening a new business, and so forth. *Health needs* drive one to spiritual power depending on the society's theory of sickness and accident. Spiritual causes and the need for harmony demand attention to spiritual power. *Security needs* include the dangers perceived when venturing into new territory or travelling, natural disasters such as floods and droughts, and the dangers of sorcery and witchcraft. *Restitution needs* deal with the prescribed ways to restore order after someone has broken the rules of society. This includes dealing with the ancestors and with other human relations. *Power needs* for situations humans cannot control or explain drive one to seek help from the spiritual realm also.

For many peoples, the world is seen as dynamic with one power pitted against another. Often, there is no sharp dividing line between sacred and secular because the material and spiritual are intertwined. Power encounters, the confrontation between two or more spiritual powers, are a common occurrence. The spiritual powers that are involved when there is a power encounter may be personal or impersonal, evil or good, within a person (demonisation) or outside the person. For Christ and the church to be relevant to life, missionaries must be aware of the active, existing spiritual powers and on what occasions they are called on for assistance.

God's design has always been to meet people where they are and then gently move them closer. With most of the world heavily involved in spiritual power activities, the initial communication of the gospel must deal with spiritual power. When people give allegiance to Christ, spiritual conflicts will arise over spiritual power for each day's needs. Since warding off the attack of evil spirits is real in the daily lives of those in spiritual-power oriented societies, the new believer needs to learn to employ the power of God to overcome (not simply placate) these spirits. The form and corporate practices of the church will need to be shaped to meet the needs felt for spiritual power. Christian theology must give creedal attention to specific areas where spiritual powers are involved. Those who convert to Christ must know in practice that the Holy Spirit within empowers them for living and confronting the spiritual powers that exist around them. In societies where spiritual powers are perceived as a cause of illness, the church needs to have in its structure a means of dealing with physical illness.

Training and preparation for working in spiritual-power oriented societies has been largely deficient. What has been most detrimental to effective mission work in regards to spiritual power is the lack of a sense of the necessity to learn about where the non-believers are in their spiritual journey. Since behaviour reflects perceived needs, it is important to investigate the meaning and function in the observance of pre-Christian ritual. This investigation makes it possible to define the needs felt for spiritual power that must be met and dealt with, in the framework of Christianity. It is always helpful for a Christian to be able to look at life through someone else's lens in order to better understand their needs and behaviour.

The shortest and most effective bridge for reaching those in spiritual-power oriented societies is simply moving their allegiance from a pagan power source to the true God. This involves little or no conversion from spiritual power to secular power. The cultural results of this change of power source are likely to be forms of Christianity that look very similar to their non-Christian predecessors, but with God as the power source. Places of meeting God and the rituals conducted, as well as the practitioners, would reflect the previous ways but would also be limited to being appropriate to biblical Christianity and using only the power of the true God.

The church must develop a reputation of dealing with both the physical and spiritual dimensions of these problems, always seeking a Christian solution. The past has shown us the dangers involved in "transplanting the church" from one society to another. The theological abstractions of the West often have very little relevance to life as people of other societies experience it. It is far better to carefully define the church and what it means to accept Christ from a scriptural base, and then let believers develop and grow as a church through God's Word and Spirit. They will find answers to their needs from the Bible, and in this way their spiritual power needs will be met.

11. A Word of Warning and Encouragement

Ricardo Barbossa de Sousa, who contributed a paper to the consultation from a Brazilian perspective, left us with a serious warning. Drawing on the teaching found in the Book of Job, he claimed that the choice for power is always a diabolic choice. That is why both Job and Jesus refused the ever so common and popular path of dualism that has the world divided between two great, equal powers that fight over the control of man and history. Our Lord reigns; that is the great announcement. Right after being violently afflicted by the catastrophes caused by Satan, Job doesn't say, "The Lord provided and Satan took, so now I should go and get back what was taken from me." On the contrary, his statement reveals that, even though Satan is the author of all the disgraces that came over Job and his family, he continued putting God at the centre of all that happened by saying, "The Lord gave, the Lord has taken away, blessed be the name of the Lord" (Job 1:21).

When we embrace dualism, spiritual war becomes a fight for power; a test to prove who is strongest and most powerful. We enter the arena created by Satan himself and end up fighting with his weapons. We opt for power, for control and fall in the great trap that Satan prepares for us. Jesus, when tempted, never used his power to prove himself to Satan, or even to the world.

One of the dangers of spiritual warfare is that we may be led to use the same weapons that Satan uses, power weapons. C.S. Lewis says that there is no spiritual war; but an internal rebellion and the rebel is under control. The power that overturned sin and Satan was the power of love, of incarnation, of deliverance, of giving. This is the weapon of our war: What Satan wanted to prove was that no one loves God for no reason, that no one searches for and serves God simply because God is God, that Job's integrity and righteousness were nothing more than a means of getting things from God and that men only truly love themselves and not God.

Our calling is to go to Calvary, to suffer all the implications of love and servitude and resist all the schemes that attempt to pull us away from following Jesus on his path to Jerusalem. Spiritual victory is the answer to unselfish and unconditional love for God and his kingdom. As long as we are righteous in our motives and desires, as long as we stick to the path of discipleship and the Cross, as long as we are obedient and submissive to the Lord and the Word, we will remain alongside the one who is, and will always be, the winner.

Because Satan knows that the victory is in Christ's incarnation, death and resurrection, his strategy is always to deny who Christ is and what he has done. Therefore, the criterion to disclose any Satanic and demonic attack or deception is the confession of Jesus Christ as the incarnate God who has, through his suffering, atoned for the sins of the world and, through his resurrection, conquered death for ever.

> "By this you know the Spirit of God: every spirit that confesses that Jesus Christ has come in flesh is from God, and every spirit that does not confess Jesus is not from God. And this is the spirit of the antichrist, of which you have heard that it is coming; and now it is already in the world" (1 John 4:2-3).

12. Consultation Statement

We conclude this paper with the official statement from the consultation. This statement was the fruit of many hours of work during the consultation by an editorial committee. It incorporates changes made through discussion time over the final day by all in attendance, and was adopted unanimously by the participants.

Introduction

Spiritual conflict is an emerging, yet uneasy, frontier in taking the whole gospel to the whole world. Enthusiasm and concern rest side by side. Trying to come to grips with the many complex issues, thirty practitioners, missiologists, pastors and theologians gathered in Nairobi, Kenya from August 16th to 22nd 2000. Together, we discussed issues of spiritual conflict in the "Consultation on Deliver Us From Evil," convened by the Lausanne Committee for World Evangelization and the Association of Evangelicals in Africa. The consultation objective was to seek a biblical and comprehensive understanding of 1) who the Enemy is; 2) how he is working; and 3) how we can fight him in order to be most effective in the evangelisation of all peoples.

Our group included practitioners of deliverance and prayer ministries from Latin America, Africa, Asia, Europe, Australia and the United States; pastors and evangelical leaders from Africa and North America; an executive of a relief and development agency; an African psychologist working in North America; theologians from Asia, Europe and North America; missionaries working in Africa and Latin America; mission executives from Europe and North America; and missiological educators from North America and Europe. Among us were Presbyterians, Pentecostals, Methodists, Anglicans, Lutherans, Baptists and members of the Evangelical Church of West Africa, Church of South India, Berachah Prophetic Church, Evangelical Covenant Church, Brethren Church, Christian and Missionary Alliance and Bible Church (United States).

We noted with interest that most of the consultation participants from Western societies had come to recognise the realities of the unseen or spiritual realm as a result of their cross-cultural experience. Those from the Two Thirds World frequently reported their experiences with Western missionaries, who were unaware of these spiritual realities, and were thus unable to minister to the spiritual realities that Two Thirds World people experience on a day-to-day basis.

As we have met in Nairobi, we have learned from the insights of sisters and brothers from East Africa and the East African revival. We particularly affirm how our East African sisters and brothers lift up Jesus and his crucifixion in the face of spiritual conflict. We realise afresh that the only way to break the power of Satan in everyday life, in society and in culture is by walking in the light so that Satan may not bind us in the darkness.

As we pray the prayer, "Deliver us from evil," we pray to be delivered from personal sin, natural evils, evil spirits and powers, and evil in society.

Origins

Our point of departure includes the Lausanne Covenant, the Manila Manifesto and the 1993 LCWE Statement on Spiritual Warfare, all of which state the reality of our engagement in spiritual conflict:

> "We believe that we are engaged in constant spiritual warfare with the principalities and powers of evil, who are seeking to overthrow the church and frustrate its task of world evangelisation." (Lausanne Covenant, 1974)

> "We affirm that spiritual warfare demands spiritual weapons, and that we must both preach the Word in the power of the Spirit and pray constantly that we may enter into Christ's victory over the principalities and powers of evil." (Manila Manifesto, 1989)

> "We agreed that evangelisation is to bring people from darkness to light and from the power of Satan to God (Acts 26:18). This involves an inescapable element of spiritual warfare." (Lausanne Statement on Spiritual Warfare, 1993)

The Consultation and participants recognise the relevance of spiritual conflict to world evangelisation. We are not trying to side with any particular view, but to expand evangelical thinking in an emerging area that has controversy. This statement indicates areas of common agreement, areas of unresolved tensions, warnings and points to areas needing further study and exploration. Our intention is to encourage churches of all traditions to use this statement to stimulate forthright discussion, serious reflection and practical ministry on spiritual conflict to the glory of God.

Common Ground

Theological Affirmations

We affirm the biblical witness that humans were created in the image of God to live in communion with the Lord, in fellowship with other humans and as stewards of God's creation. The relation between God and humankind was broken through the mysterious entry of evil into God's creation. Since the Fall, evil has influenced all aspects of the created world and human existence. It is God's plan to redeem and restore God's fallen creation. God's redemptive purpose is being revealed and realised in the history of salvation, and fully in the gospel of the incarnation, death, resurrection, ascension and return of God's son, Jesus Christ. We are called to participate in God's mission of fighting evil and the Evil One in order to restore what was destroyed as a result of the Fall. We live in a world with tension between the kingdom that has already come in Christ and the continuing realities of evil. God's mission will be completed when Christ returns, the kingdom of God comes into power, and evil is destroyed and eliminated forever.

1) Calling people to faith in Christ, inviting them to be delivered from the domain of darkness into the kingdom of God, is the missionary mandate for all Christians. We affirm a holistic understanding of evangelisation that finds its source in our relation with Christ and his call to us to become intimate with him in the fellowship of believers. The Holy Spirit empowers us for world evangelisation through the interrelated ministries of word (proclamation), deed (social service and action) and sign (miracles, power encounters), all of which take place in the context of spiritual conflict.

2) Satan is a real, personal, spiritual and created being. Satan tempted Jesus in the wilderness, sought to destroy him, and yet in light of the resurrection morning found himself defeated. Satan continues to actively oppose God's mission and the work of God's Church.[1]

3) The powers and principalities are ontologically real beings. They cannot be reduced to mere social or psychological structures.[2]

4) Satan works by taking what God has created for human well-being, and perverts it toward his purposes, which are to destroy and devalue life by enslaving individuals, families, local communities and whole societies. Satan contextualises his efforts differently in various societies and cultures.

5) Satan uses deception in an attempt to redirect human allegiances to anyone or anything other than God. In addition to the personal level, Satan does this with regard to all institutionalised forms of religious or ideological allegiance, including the church.

6) Satan and "the rulers, authorities, the powers of this dark world, the spiritual forces of evil in the heavenly realms" are at work through:[3]

   a) Deceiving and distorting;

   b) Tempting to sin;

   c) Afflicting the body, emotions, mind and will;

   d) Taking control of a person;

   e) Disordering of nature;

   f) Distorting the roles of social, economic and political strucures;

---

[1] Job 1-2; Zech 3:1; 1 Chron 21:1; Matt 4:1-11; Matt 12:23; Luke 8:12; Luke 22:3; John 12:31; 13:2; 16:11; Col 2:15-22.

[2] Mark 3:22; 1 Cor 2:6-8; 15:24-26; Col 2:15; Eph 1:21; 3:10; 6:10-18.

[3] 2 Cor 2:11; 1 Thess 3:5; 1 Tim 2:14; Rev 12:10; Matt 8:16; Matt 9:32; Mark 5:1-20; Mark 9:17; Luke 8:30; Job 2:7; Matt 9:32-33; 12:22-23; 15:22-28; Job 1:16-19.

g) Scapegoating as a means of legitimising violence;

h) Promoting self-interest, injustice, oppression and abuse;

i) The realm of the occult;

j) False religions; and

k) All forms of opposition to God's work of salvation and the mission of the church.

7) A primary purpose of the life and ministry of Jesus was to expose, confront and defeat Satan and destroy his works.

a) Christ has decisively defeated Satan at the Cross and through the resurrection.

b) Jesus confronted Satan through prayer, righteousness, obedience and setting the captives free.

c) In the ways Jesus ministered to people, he mounted an enormous challenge to the institutions and structures of the world.

d) Christians share in Christ's victory and are given the authority of Christ to stand against the attacks of Satan in the victory we have in Christ.[4]

The model for spiritual authority is Jesus and his obedience and submission to God on the Cross.

8) While we acknowledge that God is sovereignly in control of creation, the biblical evidence indicates a variety of causes of illness and calamity: God, Satan, human choices or trauma and a disordered universe are all cited. We understand that we may not know with certainty the exact cause of any particular illness or calamity.

9) The elements of a worldview that is Christian, within our respective cultural contexts, must include:

a) God is the creator and sustainer of all that exists, both seen

---

[4] John 12:31; 16:11, 33; Col 2:15; Heb 2:14; 1 John 3:8; Rev 5:5; Eph 6:10-18; James 4:7; Luke 9:1; Matt 28:18; cf Matt 12:28; Eph 6:11, 13.

and unseen. This creation includes humans and spiritual beings as moral creatures.

b) People were made in the image of God, in which the aspects of the human person are inseparably connected. Body, soul, emotions and mind cannot be separated.

c) God remains sovereign over all creation in history, and nothing happens outside God's ultimate control. Thus, the world cannot be conceived of as a closed universe governed merely by naturalistic scientific laws. Neither can it be considered a dualistic system in which Satan is understood to be equal to God.

d) Because we reject a dualistic worldview, the blessings of God and the ministrations of the angelic host, the consequences of sin and the assaults of Satan and demons cannot be isolated solely to a spiritual realm.

e) Any teaching on spiritual conflict that leads us to fear the Devil to such an extent that we lose our confidence in Christ's victory over him and in God's sovereign power to protect us must be rejected.

f) All matters concerning spiritual conflict must be viewed first and foremost in terms of our relation with and faith in God, and not simply in terms of techniques that we must master.

g) The return of Christ and the ultimate consummation of his victory over Satan gives us confidence today in dealing with spiritual struggles and a lens through which we are to interpret the events in the world today.

10) The person and work of the Holy Spirit are central in spiritual conflict:[5]

a) The empowering of the Holy Spirit, the exercise of spiritual gifts and prayer are prerequisites for engaging in spiritual conflict.

---

[5] Gal 5:21-22; 1 Cor 13:4-7; Eph 6:17.

b) The exercise of spiritual gifts must be accompanied by the fruit of the spirit.

c) The work of the Spirit and the Word must be held together.

Spiritual Conflict in Practice

1) We listened to reports on the history of the church's dealings with Satan and the demonic and noted:

a) There are striking similarities between what happened in the history of the ancient church and what is happening in demonic encounters and deliverance today.

b) Deliverance from Satanic and demonic powers and influence in the ancient church was used as proof of the resurrection and the truth of the claims of Christ by the church fathers.

c) Preparation for baptism included the renunciation of the Devil, the demonic and prior religious allegiances from the life of the convert, as well as repentance. This practice continues in some churches to this day.

d) The unwillingness or inability of the contemporary Western church to believe in the reality of the spiritual realm and engage in spiritual conflict arose out of a defective Enlightenment-influenced worldview, and is not representative of the total history of the church in relation to spiritual conflict nor has it been characteristic of Christianity in the Two Thirds World in contemporary history.

e) Every Christian has access to the authority of Christ and demons recognise Christ's power when exercised by Christians.

f) The history of evangelism is replete with examples in which the response to the gospel was accompanied by power encounters, but power encounters in and of themselves are never a guarantee of a positive response.

g) Church history also points to a link between idolatry and the demonic.

2) Working for positive strongholds for God through a "gentle invasion" that overcomes evil with good and wins people by love is as important as breaking down Satanic strongholds. Thus, we affirm the importance and primacy of the local church and its life of faith.

3) Worship is spiritual conflict. It is not aggressive, spectacular spiritual conflict; not a strategy nor a means to an end; but involves mind, body and spirit responding with all that we are, to all that God is.

4) Spiritual conflict is risky and often costly. While there are victories, there is often a backlash from the Evil One in various forms of attack such as illness and persecution. Nonetheless, we do not shrink from spiritual conflict, since to avoid it is costly to the kingdom of God.

5) The ministry of spiritual conflict is grounded in the transformative power of relations, not techniques or methods.

6) The point of departure for spiritual conflict is our relation with Jesus and listening to the Holy Spirit.

7) We affirm the complexity of the human person. We need to distinguish the psychological from the spiritual when it comes to ministry and counselling. Deliverance ministries and psychological counsellors often fail to recognise this distinction. Failure to do so can do harm.

8) Holiness is central to the Christian response to evil:

   a) In the exercise of spiritual authority, those who do not give adequate attention to character and holiness truncate the whole biblical picture of spiritual growth and sanctification.

   b) To practice spiritual conflict without adequate attention to personal holiness is to invite disaster.

   c) The pursuit of holiness applies not only to the individual, but to the family, the local church and the larger community of faith.

   d) While holiness includes personal piety, it applies to social relations as well.

9) Engaging the Evil One is not the work for heroic individuals. Those engaged in this ministry must seek the support of a group of intercessors.

10) Following up on individuals who have experienced freedom through spiritual conflict must be an inseparable part of the ministry. The local church must be encouraged to incorporate people into the Christian community and to disciple them; not to arrange for this is sin.

11) We were saddened by stories of people, emboldened by self-assured certainty and money, who come from outside, over-whelm local Christians and carry out hit-and-run ministries of spiritual conflict that 1) presume superior knowledge of the local reality; 2) treat local Christians as inferior or unaware, 3) claim credit for things that local Christians have been praying and working toward for years and 4) leave uneven results and sometimes pain, alienation and even persecution of the local church, while claiming great victory.

12) Spiritual conflict involves more than one enemy; it must engage the flesh, the Devil and the world:

a) We view with alarm social evils such as injustice, poverty, ethnocentrism, racism, genocide, violence, environmental abuse, wars, as well as the violence, pornography and occult in the media.

b) These social evils are encouraged or supported by human institutions in which the principalities and powers work against God and God's intention for humankind.

c) The task of the church in combating the principalities and powers in the socio-political context is to unmask their idolatrous pretensions, to identify their dehumanising values and actions and to work for the release of their victims. This work involves spiritual, political and social actions.

13) We fail to find biblical warrant for constructing elaborate hierarchies of the spirit world.

Warnings

1) We urge caution and sensitivity in the use of language when it comes to spiritual conflict. While biblical, the term *spiritual warfare* is offensive to non-Christians and carries connotations that seem contradictory coming from those who serve a Lord who died on a cross. Additionally, there is a large range of meanings attached to various spiritual conflict terms such as healing, deliverance, power encounters, possession, demonisation, powers and so on. Also, new terms are constantly being coined (eg, Strategic Level Spiritual Warfare, deep-level healing, etc.).

2) We call for watchfulness to avoid any syncretism with non-Christian religious beliefs and practices, such as traditional religions or new religious movements. We also affirm that new believers are reasonable when they expect the gospel to meet their needs for spiritual power.

3) We call for discernment concerning magical uses of Christian terms and caution practitioners to avoid making spiritual conflict into Christian magic. Any suggestion that a particular technique or method in spiritual-conflict ministry ensures success is a magical, sub-Christian understanding of God's workings.

4) We encourage extreme care and the discernment of the community to ensure that the exercise of spiritual authority not become spiritual abuse. Any expression of spiritual power or authority must be done in compassion and love.

5) We cry out for a mantle of humility and gracefulness on the part of cross-cultural workers, who having recently discovered the reality of the spirit realm, go to other parts of the world where people have known and lived with the local realities of the spirit world and the struggle with the demonic for centuries.

6) Because spiritual conflict is expressed in different ways in different societies, we strongly caution against taking ideas, methods or strategies developed in one society and using them uncritically in another.

7) Because we must resist the temptation to adopt the Devil's tactics as our own, we warn practitioners to take care that their methods in spiritual conflict are based on the work of Christ on the cross:

   a) Submitting to God through his substitutionary death on the cross, Christ deprived Satan of his claim to power;

   b) Christ's willingness to sacrifice himself, in contrast to fighting back, is a model for spiritual conflict; and

   c) When we separate the Cross from spiritual conflict, we create a climate of triumphalism.

8) We call for actions that ensure that our approaches and explanations of spiritual conflict do not tie new converts to the very fears from which Christ died to free them. Being free in Christ means being free from fear of the demonic.

9) We warn against an overemphasis on spirits that blame demons for the actions of people. Demons can only work through people — and people can actively choose to co-operate. Spirits are not the *only* source of resistance to the gospel.

10) We warn against confusing correlations or coincidence with causation in reporting apparent victories as well as the uncritical use of undocumented accounts to establish the validity of cosmic warfare.

11) We warn against using eschatology as an excuse not to fight against all forms of evil in the present.

Areas of Tension

1) In the early church, demonic encounters were most often seen where the church encountered non-Christians. The history of evangelisation frequently links power encounters with the evangelisation of non-Christian people. The biblical text reveals that while it is possible that a demonic spirit may afflict a believer physically,[6] there is no direct evidence that demons need

---

[6] Luke 4:38-39; 13:10-13; 2 Cor 12:7-9.

to be cast out of believers. On the other hand, we also heard the testimony of brothers and sisters from every continent to the contrary. This raises the question of how we are to understand the effect of the demonic in the lives of Christians. We were unable to resolve this tension in our consultation, but believe the following are helpful to note:

a) We are aware that in many cases, new Christians today have not gone through processes of renunciation of pre-Christian allegiances, processes that have been normative in the pre-Enlightenment Church. Some Christians may have lost their faith; there are others who call themselves Christians, but are only Christians in a nominal sense. Some claim that these might be reasons that Christians might appear to be susceptible to the demonic.

b) We affirm that being in Christ means the Christian belongs to Christ and that our nature is transformed. However, just as with sin and our need to deal with sin in our body, mind, emotions and will, we wonder if the demonic, while no longer able to claim ownership of Christians, may not continue to afflict them in body, mind, emotions and will unless dealt with.

2) While it is possible that Satan manifests himself more strongly in certain places than in others, and that some spirits seem to be tied to certain locations, we agreed there seems to be little biblical warrant for a number of the teachings and practices associated with some forms of spiritual conflict which focus on territorial spirits. We experienced tension over whether there is biblical warrant for prayer warfare against territorial spirits as a valid tool for evangelisation. We agreed, however, on the invalidity of the claim that prayer warfare against territorial spirits is *the* only key to effective evangelisation.

3) Tension exists concerning the extent to which we can learn and verify things from the spiritual realm from experiences not immediately verifiable from Scripture, in contrast to limiting our understanding of the spiritual realm from Scripture alone. Some have maintained that experience is crucial to understanding

spiritual conflict; this is a point to be explored in ongoing dialogue.

4) We are not agreed as to whether or how the truths about spiritual realities and spiritual conflict methodologies can be verified empirically. Some engage in active experimentation in spiritual-conflict ministry as a means of developing generalities concerning spiritual conflict, while others are not convinced of the validity of this way of learning.

Frontiers That Need Continued Exploration

1) While affirming the Lausanne position on the Bible, there is an urgent need for a hermeneutic that:

   a) Allows culture and experience to play a role in the formulation of our understanding and theology of spiritual conflict. The basis and test of such a theology is Scripture, as faithfully interpreted by the Spirit-guided hermeneutical community of the global church.

   b) Allows an examination of issues that arise in Christian experience not directly addressed in Scripture.

   c) Accepts the fact that the Holy Spirit has surprised the church by acting in ways not explicitly taught in Scriptures (Acts 10 and 15) and may be doing so again.

2) There is an urgent need to incorporate the study of spiritual conflict into theological curricula in schools and training centres around the world.

3) There is an urgent need to develop criteria and methods that allow us to evaluate ministry experience in a verifiable way.

4) The emerging understanding of the complexity of the human person needs significant exploration and examination. Specifically, we call for:

   a) A sustained dialogue between those engaged in deliverance ministries and those in the medical and psychological professions;

b) Urgent sharing worldwide with deliverance practitioners of the current state of knowledge of Dissociative Identity Disorder (DID), formerly called Multiple Personality Disorder;

c) A diagnostic approach that allows practitioners to discern the difference between DID personalities and spiritual entities; and

d) A dialogue between theologians and the medical and psychological professions that develops a holistic understanding of the human person, inseparably relating body, mind, emotions and spirit as they function individually and relationally.

5) We call for a more interdisciplinary approach to the description of spiritual conflict, drawing on the insights of relevant disciplines.

6) We call on the churches to develop an understanding of sanctification that addresses all of the human person: our spiritual, emotional, mental and physical selves. Such a holistic understanding of sanctification will include the development of spiritual disciplines, inner healing and deliverance. All need to become tools supporting the sanctification of Christians through the Word by the Holy Spirit.[7]

7) There is a need to explore the role in spiritual conflict of the practices of Baptism, Holy Communion, confession of sin and absolution, footwashing and anointing with oil.

8) We would like to see a serious examination of the deception and the seductive power of advertising in terms of its role in fostering envy, consumerism and false gods.

We praise God, that while we represented various theological, cultural and church traditions and positions on spiritual conflict, we have been blessed and inspired by learning from each other. This encourages us to believe that it is possible to develop an understanding of spiritual conflict and its practice within the Christian

---

[7] John 15:3; 17:17.

community, so that in time it becomes part of the everyday life of the church. We invite the church to join us in continued study and in the incorporation of appropriate ministries of spiritual conflict into the life of the church. We particularly call on the churches in the West to listen more carefully to the churches in the Two Thirds World and join them in a serious rediscovery of the reality of evil.

Appendix A: List of Participants

Tokunboh Adeyemo, Kenya (Co-Convener)

Mary Aruwa, Kenya

David Burnett, United Kingdom

Paul A. Cedar, United States

Robyn Claydon, Australia

Jacson Homero Eberhardt, Brazil

Tormod Engelsviken, Norway

Ezekiah Francis, India

David Gitari, Kenya

Grace Anzaye, Kenya

Deborah Hendrickson, Kenya

Yung Hwa, Malaysia

Neuza Itioka, Brazil

Margaret Jacobs, Western Australia

Knud Jørgensen, Norway (Co-Convener)

Ken Kimiywe, Kenya

Charles Kraft, United States

Marguerite Kraft, United States

Ole Skjerbæk Madsen, Denmark

Wilson Mamboleo, Kenya

Kaare Melhus, Norway

Scott Moreau, United States

Jerry Mungadze, United States

Bryant Myers, United States

Birger Nygaard, Denmark

Olusegun Olanipekun, Kenya

Heinrich Christian Rust, Germany

Lars Råmunddal, Norway

Chris Thomas, United States

Juliet Thomas, India

Yusufu Turaki, Nigeria

Contributing Authors in Absentia:

Ricardo Barbossa de Sousa, Brazil

Oskar Skarsaune, Norway

Amsalu Tadesse, Ethiopia

Appendix B: What is Lausanne?

"Making Christ known together"

- Lausanne was a congress called by a committee headed by the Reverend Billy Graham in 1974 in the beautiful city of Lausanne, Switzerland. Christian leaders attended from 150 countries and many denominations.

- Lausanne gave its name to a covenant which, for over 25 years, has challenged churches and Christian organisations to do a better job of making Jesus known in the world.

- Lausanne continues to organise consultations and conferences, publish newsletters and books, and in other ways encourage the work of world evangelisation.

- Lausanne is a volunteer network of individuals and groups who affirm the Lausanne Covenant and who are committed to support the work of world evangelisation, wherever it is done in a way that is true to the Bible.

- Lausanne's network has about 25 committees in different countries and regions of the world.

- Lausanne is supported financially by the people in its network and by the gifts of those who believe in its work.

Lausanne believes...

- that co-operation and sharing in world evangelisation is better than competition;

- that the whole gospel will include demonstration by deeds as well as proclamation by words;

- that biblical theology and mission strategy must be consistent; and

- that its own neutrality creates space for all evangelicals to work together regardless of their church or faith tradition.

Lausanne organizes...

- small international consultations on subjects that are critical to completing the task of world evangelisation. These bring together key people in order to achieve an approach which is biblical and strategic. There have been more than 30 of these.

- regional, national and international consultations and conferences where a need for these is expressed. There have been more than 50 of these.

- world congresses (1974 and 1989) that bring together current and emerging leaders to consider world evangelisation.

Lausanne publishes...

- the occasional Lausanne Newsletter with news and analyses of current issues arising for those who want to make Christ known to the world; and

- occasional papers and books on subjects important for world evangelisation.

A *"Barnabas Factor"*

Lausanne is a "Barnabas factor" in the church. It encourages churches:

- to trust new and younger leaders;

- to undertake work among people different from themselves; and

- to stay with people who have different ideas until they find each other in a new way (Acts 9:27, 11:22-26, 15:36-39).

Lausanne Occasional Papers available:

LOP 27   Modern, Postmodern and Christian
         US$4.95

LOP 28   Ministry in Islamic Contexts
         US$6.50

LOP 29   Spiritual Conflict in Today's Mission
         US$7.95

Available from:
World Vision Publications
800 West Chestnut Avenue
Monrovia, California
91016-3198
U.S.A.
Tel: 001-626-301-7720   1-800-777-7752 (U.S.)
Fax: 001-626-301-7789
www.marcpublications.com